LAW FORUM SERIES

College of Law, Ohio State University

TWO STUDIES IN
CONSTITUTIONAL INTERPRETATION

TWO STUDIES IN
CONSTITUTIONAL INTERPRETATION

Search, Seizure, and Surveillance

and

Fair Trial and Free Press

TELFORD TAYLOR

Ohio State University Press

Columbus, Ohio

1969

KF
9625
.T3

FOREWORD

THE TWO ESSAYS which comprise this volume are based on lectures presented on April 3 and 4, 1967 at the College of Law of Ohio State University, as part of the annual Law Forum Series. Each of them has been expanded—the first considerably and the second slightly—and annotated. The lectures were delivered extemporaneously from an outline; the wording of these essays is derived from a tape recording. I have ironed out the roughest spots, but have not sought to eliminate the oral quality.

During the year that passed between the presentation at Ohio State and the completion of the written text, there were several important Supreme Court decisions in the field of search and seizure, and significant changes were made in the ABA recommendations on "Fair Trial and Free Press." Rather than revise the text itself to encompass this after-acquired matter, I have added a postscript to each essay.

I am deeply grateful to the faculty of the Law School, and especially to Professor Merton C. Bernstein, for honoring me with the invitation and for their many kindnesses in connection with my visit to Ohio State and the publication of this volume. I am also indebted to Miss Marian Halley and Mr. Jeffrey S. Tallackson, students at the Columbia Law School, for helpful research in connection with the essay on search and seizure.

April, 1968   TELFORD TAYLOR

CONTENTS

Contents

Introduction

INTRODUCTION

A LITTLE OVER A YEAR AGO I had the honor and pleasure of representing the State of New York in the Supreme Court of the United States, for argument as friend of the court in the now famous *Miranda* cases [1] on pre-arraignment interrogation of suspects in police custody. While in court, I heard argument in one of those cases [2] presented by the Honorable William I. Siegel, Assistant District Attorney of Kings County, New York. In the course of his argument, Mr. Siegel declared that there was "an old common law right to stop a person and detain him for a reasonable period of time for discussion and investigation. I don't think that has ever been disputed." [3]

Mr. Siegel did not have to wait long for dispute to develop: the Chief Justice promptly asked him whether "this Court has ever said you could put men in jail and hold them there during the investigation of the police, unless the police arrest him for proper cause?" Mr. Siegel replied that he "thought the right has been recognized," and then remarked that "there is a whole model code on the right to detain, in preparation"—referring to the American Law Institute Model Code of Pre-Arraignment Procedure,[4] which is indeed in preparation.

Mr. Justice Black, who had not been sympathetic to Mr. Siegel's argument, immediately interjected: "What

3

is that Model Code? Is that in the Constitution?" His question was rhetorical and contentious, and Mr. Siegel made a quick shift to another branch of his argument. I confess that I did not then and there think of anything better that Mr. Siegel could have done.

But, as is all too often the case, other thoughts come to mind after the crucial moment of advocacy has passed. In retrospect, I believe that Mr. Justice Black's question should have been answered somewhat as follows: "In the only sense in which your Honor's question is meaningful, the answer is 'yes.' Of course the Code is not within the four corners of the document signed in 1787 or of any of the amendments, but that is so obvious that it cannot be what your Honor really meant. It would be difficult to find a single Supreme Court opinion on an important constitutional question which has relied exclusively on the language of the Constitution, because invariably the language of the disputed portions is general, and other guides to its interpretation and application must be found. These other guides are part of the process of constitutional adjudication, and in that sense—the only sense relevant to your Honor's question—they are part of the Constitution. The issue, therefore, is whether a contemporary document such as the American Law Institute Code may be of relevant import in construing the Bill of Rights, and I repeat that the answer to that question should be 'yes.' "

I have described this episode not because the *Miranda* case is directly relevant to either of my subjects, but because Justice Black's question and the reflections it stimulates seem to me basic to many if not most problems of constitutional interpretation. And before embarking on the two particular studies here in prospect, it is appropriate for me to indicate, as best I can, some interpretive factors to which I would give weight.

About the institution of judicial review itself, I shall speak only summarily. I do not share the doubts about the legitimacy of that institution that have been expressed by the late Judge Learned Hand,[5] and others of considerable if not equal eminence.[6] I believe that the language and history of the Constitution abundantly support the proposition that legislative, executive, and judicial action are subject to final judicial scrutiny in constitutional terms. In general I agree with my distinguished colleague, Herbert Wechsler, that the scrutiny should be principled.[7] But the rigor of insistence on judicial principle must, I believe, be tempered by awareness that the Court is a political institution, and that judicial review will survive only as long as the Court does not cut too sharply athwart the stream of political power, wherever the sources of that power may be found.[8]

Principled constitutional decision requires a principled concept of the Constitution as an entity, and this leads us back to Mr. Justice Black's question and the answer I have suggested. Does the Constitution speak as of yesterday, today, or tomorrow? By what temporal standards are its words to be measured? Does the Constitution mean what it was meant to mean, or what it has come to mean, or what it ought to mean? Are these alternatives mutually exclusive, or may they be used in combination or according to circumstance? These are among the questions which closely hedge the path to constitutional decision.

As you all know, these questions are especially germane to the Court's chronic disagreement over the relation between the Bill of Rights and the due process clause of the fourteenth amendment, and thus to determining the extent of which the Bill of Rights, *via* the fourteenth amendment, limits the states. In conducting his campaign for "total incorporation" of the Bill of Rights, Mr. Justice Black emerged twenty years ago as principal judicial spokesman for the view that the Constitution means what it was meant to mean. Accordingly, he based his "total incorporation" theory on a historical study intended to show that this is what was meant at the time the fourteenth amendment was adopted.[9]

It would be less than just to this view—emphasizing as it does the "original understanding" of the framers—to condemn it as narrow literalism, bound by the meaning of words at the time they were written. When the Constitution forbids the states to "keep Troops, or Ships of War in time of Peace," [10] that must today be taken to include military aircraft as well; a contrary conclusion would be constitutional madness. Nor does the "original understanding" approach necessarily exclude empirical evidence; one can, for example, be as "absolute" as one pleases about the first amendment, and yet there may still remain a question whether a given law does in fact have a repressive effect on speech. Mr. Justice Black has himself recognized the constitutional relevance of such factual inquiries *dehors* the wording of the document.[11]

Nevertheless, the "original understanding" view leads to serious difficulties when the general guaranties of the Constitution are brought into question. The Bill of Rights, for example, does not say that an accused shall have the right to testify in his own defense, for the very good reason that in 1789, and for over half a century thereafter, he had no such right. During the second half of the nineteenth century, all the states with the exception of Georgia changed the rule and granted the right. But Georgia clung to the old ways, and in 1961 a case involving the constitutionality of Georgia's denial of an accused's right to testify reached the Supreme Court.

Reversing the conviction, Mr. Justice Brennan declared that it had become the "considered consensus of the English-speaking world" that the old rule had no rational basis.[12] There is no doubt but that the Georgia statute would have been declared unconstitutional, except for a procedural gimmick of dubious validity which enabled the Court to reverse the conviction on the ground that the defendant had been denied the "assistance of counsel" guaranteed by the sixth amendment.[13] Failing such an escape hatch, how could the Georgia statute be invalidated other than by giving the due process clause a meaning which it certainly did not have in 1789 or, for that matter, in 1868?

Mr. Justice Brennan's reference to a "considered consensus" suggests that the Constitution means what it has come to mean. In that case Mr. Justice Black voiced no reservations, but in other contexts he has inveighed mightily against the notion of a temporally flexible content of the due process clause, describing it, in his notable

7

dissent in the Connecticut birth control case, as a "natural law due process philosophy which many . . . opinions repudiated, and which I cannot accept." [14]

Mr. Justice Black was the first Roosevelt appointee to a Court which for years had been marshalling majorities to strike down social legislation under the due process clause. It may well be that his views were initially shaped, at least in part, by his desire to narrow the scope of the due process clause and thus broaden the permissible range of legislative action. But that war was won soon after he ascended the bench; nevertheless, today he still sees enduring values in a restricted permissible range of constitutional interpretation. In the perspective of history and the shifting sands of judicial personnel, his cautions are not to be lightly disregarded.

But despite Mr. Justice Black's protests, the "considered consensus" has provided a basis for many of the Court's recent decisions, including some in the field of criminal procedure which have been among those most sharply criticized. It is, I think, not sufficiently realized that, with few exceptions, the U.S. Supreme Court has not stepped out in front of the state courts and legislatures but has followed their lead. At the time of the *Gideon* case,[15] all but a dozen states provided trial counsel for indigent defendants, and all but five did so in felony cases.[16] At the time of *Griffin* v. *California*,[17] all but six states barred comment on a defendant's failure to testify.[18] The *Mapp* case [19] probably provoked as loud a cry of outrage as any decision of the last decade, but in fact the exclusionary rule for unlawfully seized evidence was born not in the

District of Columbia but in Iowa,[20] and when the *Mapp* case was decided, although the states were about evenly divided, the trend toward exclusion was unmistakeable.[21] Even the ruling in the *Escobedo* case [22] had been anticipated by the Court of Appeals of my own state of New York.[23]

But the *Miranda* case cannot be justified either on the basis of "original understanding" or of "considered consensus." By no stretch of history can it be seriously contended that either the privilege against self-incrimination or the right to the assistance of counsel, as those clauses were understood in 1791, prevented the pre-arraignment interrogation of suspects.[24] Nor had any State previously adopted the rules laid down in Chief Justice Warren's opinion.[25]

Accordingly, in my view, the *Miranda* case is strikingly illustrative of the third approach that I have mentioned: to wit, that the Constitution means what it ought to mean. Perhaps that is why the key passage of the Chief Justice's opinion suggests the legislative rather than the judicial mind at work. I need hardly add that it is not my present purpose either to praise or condemn the substantive content of the *Miranda* rules.

Another factor of possible relevance to our inquiry has been most clearly articulated by the late Mr. Justice Frankfurter in his dissenting opinion in the *Lovett* case, decided in 1946.[26] In that case Congress had added to an appropriation bill a rider barring the future disbursement of federal funds to three named civil servants. The Court held this provision unconstitutional as a Bill of

9

Attainder. Dissenting, Justice Frankfurter essayed a distinction between words of specific and words of general import: [27]

Broadly speaking, two types of constitutional claims come before this Court. Most constitutional issues derive from the broad standards of fairness written into the Constitution (*e.g.*, "due process," "equal protection of the laws," "just compensation"), and the division of power as between States and Nation. Such questions, by their very nature, allow a relatively wide play for individual legal judgment. The other class gives no such scope. For the second class of constitutional issues derives from very specific provisions of the Constitution. These had their source in definite grievances and led the Fathers to proscribe against recurrence of their experience. These specific grievances and the safeguards against their recurrence were not defined by the Constitution. They were defined by history. Their meaning was so settled by history that definition was superfluous. Judicial enforcement of the Constitution must respect these historic limits.

The Constitution, to be sure, is not all of a piece. When we read that there shall be two senators from each state or that the President must be thirty-five years of age, these numerical adjectives are about as precise as words can be, whereas "due process of law" scales the heights of generality. Old phrases of art such as "Bill of Attainder" lie somewhere between, but I doubt that this one is as exact as Justice Frankfurter suggested. To trace the development of attainder from the old English statutes which imposed criminal sanctions on named individuals,[28] to the post-Civil War cases requiring oaths of past loyalty as qualifications for holding office,[29] and to the most recent Court decision invalidating the Landrum-Griffin law against

Introduction

simultaneous Communist membership and union membership,[30] is to lose one's way in the twilight zone between attainder and the denial of equal protection.[31]

As a general proposition, however, Mr. Justice Frankfurter's line of demarcation is not without merit. Whatever a bill of attainder may or may not be, it is not a letter of marque and reprisal. The Constitution not infrequently employs legal words of art such as "treason," "felony," "habeas corpus," "warrant," and "indictment." Much as the contours of such expressions may tend to crumble under rigorous scrutiny, they are undeniably less general than "due process of law," or "freedom of speech." Accordingly, I should think it sound, in dealing with a phrase thus closely measured in historical terms, to stick fairly near to the "original understanding" of its meaning.

In the light of this far from adequate survey, we may return to Mr. Justice Black's question. He and Mr. Justice Frankfurter were early members of the Supreme Court of modern times—the Court born of the New Deal, the Court-packing plan, and the economic depression of the 1930's. They sat together on the Court for a quarter of a century, and of all its members during those years they were the leaders as sources of constitutional doctrine; among all the others there were none more deeply principled than these two, in the sense that their principles led to their results rather than the reverse.

It is, therefore, despite a profound admiration for Mr. Justice Black and his contribution to the judicial process that I venture the opinion that his quest for precision in the Bill of Rights and the fourteenth amendment is a vain one. One can, to be sure, give the due process clause specific content, as did Mr. Justice Curtis a century ago,[32] by reference to the "settled usages and modes of proceeding existing in the common law of England" at the time, but Mr. Justice Black would be the first to reject this solution.[33] His own view that the fourteenth amendment embraces the entire Bill of Rights, but nothing else unless found in some other constitutional provision,[34] pretty well shuts us out of substantive due process but gives us little guidance in the procedural area, for the Bill of Rights is cast in general terms and includes its own due process clause in the fifth amendment. To cope with the imprecision of constitutional language, Mr. Justice Black at times resorts to historical fictions or to verbal renderings which seem to me strained or over-particularized—for example, his reliance in the *Miranda* case on the word "compelled" in the self-incrimination clause to support a construction that covers all interrogation (lacking counsel or a waiver of counsel) of a person in custody.[35]

Of course I cannot provide explicit proof that the framers of the Constitution meant to endow its general expressions with a content conformable to changing times. It is a mistake to talk about the intention of the framers as if they had but one mind among them; no doubt they would have spoken to this point in great variety. But the temper of the document, the arguments in the Federalist papers and other contemporaneous discussion, the action of the early Congresses and the language of the early opinions are all to me instinct with the notion of a charter intended to preserve certain values through, and in spite of, changing circumstances in the future. I think that the framers meant the Constitution to mean more than it says, and more than they could conceive; and I think that this is part of what John Marshall meant in his famous truism about expounding a constitution.[36]

To be sure, this problem of temporal standards has not always been of such significance as it is today. When Marshall and Story wrote, the Philadelphia Convention lay well within living memory. It was altogether natural that the intent of the framers at once became the touchstone of interpretation, though Marshall and the other justices of his time relied mostly upon verbal exegesis rather than "legislative history" to ascertain that intent.[37] So too, when the Court first approached the great issues of interpretation posed by the fourteenth amendment, it was the intent of the framers of this and its two sister amendments (the thirteenth and fifteenth) which the Court found determinative.[38] It is hardly surprising, therefore, to find Mr. Justice Miller, in behalf of a unanimous Court in 1887, laying down the test of "original understanding" in categorical terms: [39]

It is never to be forgotten that, in the construction of the language of the Constitution here relied on, as indeed in all other instances where construction becomes necessary, we are to place ourselves as nearly as possible in the condition of the men who framed that instrument.

The fourteenth amendment is now one hundred years old, and none of the amendments of this century is the focus of major problems of interpretation. There is an attractive but, I believe, a spurious simplicity in the notion that the constitutional problems of today are soluble by total immersion in the "conditions" under which the framers wrote. At least within the ambit of magnificent generalizations such as "due process" and "equal protection," the "original understanding" must be leavened by the "considered consensus."

No doubt there are dangers in this view, and as a savage reminder we need only recall the Nazi concept of crime as embracing things contrary to the "healthy feeling of the people." The consensus may not be "considered"; it may be hasty and oppressive or worse, and of course it is the prime function of a Constitution to guard against these very hazards.

But if we do not want a rubber Constitution, neither do we want a rusty one. The phrase "cruel and unusual punishment," for example, is lifted verbatim from the Declaration of Right of 1688.[40] Its content did not inhibit Lord Ellenborough in 1803 from condemning a treason convict to a hanging which did not kill, but was merely the prelude to a wretched death by fire and the knife at the foot of the scaffold.[41] Perhaps the Congressmen of 1789 who proposed the eighth amendment would have been greatly surprised to see their handiwork invoked by four justices (including Mr. Justice Black) to bar the conviction of a narcotics addict,[42] but I can hardly take seriously a view which would confine that amendment's mandate by the standards of 1791. As Chief Justice Warren has written of this very clause, it "must draw its meaning from the evolving standards of decency that mark the progress of maturing society."[43] So, too, as Mr. Justice Douglas wrote more recently[44] in interpreting the Equal Protec-

14

tion Clause, "we have never been confined to historic notions of equality, any more than we have restricted due process to a fixed category of what was at a given time deemed to be the limits of fundamental rights. . . . Notions of what constitutes equal treatment for purposes of the Equal Protection Clause *do* change."

All this is surely not to say that the history and original "meaning" of the Constitution is irrelevant to its construction. On the contrary, such inquiry may yield the clearest view of the values which a particular provision was intended to protect. To achieve its basic purposes, however, the language "must be capable of wider application than the mischief that give it birth." [45]

In the course of time, once-respected practices come to be seen as mischiefs, as in the case of the disqualification of an accused as his own witness. So too, some things once condemned become tolerable. In applying the general language of the Constitution to new problems or old ones newly viewed, consensus has its place. As a manifestation of considered, professional consensus, so do the deliberations of the American Law Institute, and that is why I believe that Mr. Justice Black's question should have been answered in the affirmative.

The answer I have suggested is as good an indication as I can give of the interpretive preconceptions with which I approach the ensuing studies.

Part I: Search, Seizure, and Surveillance

Search, Seizure, and Surveillance

TEMPORAL STANDARDS of constitutional interpretation are highly relevant to the topic of the evening, for even more than its fellows, the fourth amendment was the product of particular events that closely preceded the Constitution and the Bill of Rights. Thanks especially to James Otis, John Wilkes, and Lords Camden and Mansfield, we know a good deal about the "original understanding" of those who framed the constitutional safeguards against unreasonable searches and seizures, and can find specified in the pages of history the abuses against which the fourth amendment was particularly directed.

In the immediate present, however, old habits and notions of personal privacy—whether of saints or sinners—are in grave danger of burial under an avalanche of new surveillance devices. Many of these require little or nothing by way of physical trespass for their successful operation, and most of them are designed for the remote scrutiny of future acts or speech rather than the identification of existing physical objects. The constitutional problems raised by the employment of these devices, especially in the detection of crime, are unlikely to yield readily to Mr. Justice Miller's formula,[1] and it may be equally difficult to discover Mr. Justice Brennan's "considered consensus"[2] in the welter of conflicting opinions that clamor for attention.[3]

The current importance of these questions has been greatly magnified by the *Mapp* case,[4] which, by extending to the states the rule excluding unlawfully seized evidence, turned the fourth amendment into a provision of dominant significance throughout the American judicial system. Largely as a result of the *Mapp* case, a number of the states have enacted statutes authorizing the issuance of search warrants to seize anything constituting evidence of crime, and these statutes raise new and difficult questions of law and policy to which the Supreme Court is now directing its attention after a lapse of over forty years.[5]

For the constitutional lawyer, the Supreme Court has been, with respect to the fourth amendment issues, in a state of exceptionally interesting unpredictability. In large part this is because Mr. Justice Black, who on most issues of criminal procedure is likely to support the constitutional claims of the defendant, has usually come down on the side of the police where searches and seizures are in question. Indeed, in the *Mapp* case the defendant won Mr. Justice Black's vote (crucial to the decision) not on the basis of the fourth amendment "standing alone," but only when "considered together with the Fifth Amendment's ban against compelled self-incrimination." [6]

About the *Mapp* case itself I have very little to say. Apart from expressing a belief that it is here to stay, I will only venture a reminder that the Court's division in the case, sharp as it was, did not concern the merits of the exclusionary rule. The disagreement concerned only the federal dimension of the constitutional question: should the states be left free to apply or not to apply the exclusionary rule according to state law? That is the issue on which the justices divided, and there is not a word in the dissenting opinions suggesting that the rule is intrinsically bad. Especially in view of the pre-*Mapp* trend in the state courts, I should think it likely that the case will weather even substantial changes in the Court's membership.

Four Propositions

With the *Mapp* case in the books and the practical importance of the fourth amendment thus magnified manyfold, I propose tonight to advance four general propositions.

The first concerns the search warrant and its proper place in the scheme of things. With increasing frequency one hears it said and sees it written, whether in judicial opinions or law reviews, that the warrant is of supreme importance to the validity of a search—that, with rare exceptions, searches with warrants are good and searches without warrants are bad. I propose to show that this view is in dissonance with the teaching of history, and has led to an inflation of the warrant out of all proportion to its real importance in practical terms.

In the second place, I wish to discuss the rule that I have already mentioned as once again under Supreme Court scrutiny—the rule that evidence *qua* evidence is not a legitimate object of a search or seizure. It is my position that this rule has no sound historical basis, that it no longer serves any intelligible purpose, and that, at least in its present form, it should be abandoned.

Third, I will examine some of the consequences suggested by abandoning that rule, and will propose a new look at the general question of what things may or may not be legitimate objects of search and subjects of seizure. Especially I have in mind testimonial documents, in connection with which principles and values arising out of the first and fifth amendments come into play, and preclude consideration in terms of the fourth amendment alone.

Finally, I will consider several aspects of wire-tapping and other forms of surveillance. A principal subject of my discussion will be the statutes enacted in New York and a few other states, and the bills recently considered by congressional committees, most of which provide for limited surveillance authorized by a court order which is intended to serve much the same purpose as a search warrant. I believe that the attempted analogy between such orders and search warrants is a mistaken one, both historically and in the present; that the proposed surveillance orders raise important constitutional difficulties; and that the practical value of such orders, as safeguards against oppressive surveillance, is illusory.

Bernard Shaw's play *Too True to Be Good* begins with a prologue spoken by a character called "the Microbe." At the conclusion of his speech the Microbe directly addresses the audience with the information that "the play is now virtually over, but the actors will discuss it at length for three more acts." Ladies and gentlemen, the exits are all well lighted.

Search, Seizure, and Surveillance

Searches and Warrants

An otherwise excellent note in a recent issue of the *Columbia Law Review* commences with a declaration that: [7] "The fourth amendment generally prohibits searches without warrants." In so expressing himself, the author had abundant judicial support, both in prevailing [8] and dissenting [9] opinions. Mr. Justice Frankfurter waged a vigorous campaign for the view that ". . . with minor and severely confined exceptions . . . every search and seizure is unreasonable when made without a magistrate's authority expressed through a validly issued warrant." [10] Mr. Justice Jackson, indeed, was prepared to hold that, lacking a valid warrant, there could be no lawful search whatever of premises or property.[11]

Exaltation of the warrant as the touchstone of "reasonableness" is not confined to the bench. In a recent study of the fourth amendment, conducted under distinguished professional sponsorship, surprise is expressed that the clause is not explicit to this effect: [12]

The Fourth Amendment . . . is somewhat strangely constructed. It consists of two conjunctive clauses. . . . But the Amendment nowhere connects the two clauses; it nowhere says in terms what one might expect it to say: that all searches without a warrant issued in compliance with the conditions specified in the second clause are *eo ipso* unreasonable under the first.

I will come presently to the question whether this view, eminent as are its spokesmen, corresponds at all to the realities of life in the world of law enforcement. From a historical standpoint, I believe, Mr. Justice Frankfurter and the others of like mind have stood the fourth amend-

23

ment on its head. And since the history of searches and warrants is important for other parts of my thesis, I crave your indulgence for a brief trip into the past.

History of Search Warrants

The trip will take us into a foggy land, for this is an area in which the historical scholars have not done very well for us. This murk has plagued our remote predecessor brethren of the bench and bar; two centuries ago Lord Camden complained that search warrants "crept into the law by imperceptible practice," [13] and their very legitimacy was questioned by Lord Coke.[14]

Legitimate or not, search warrants seem to be here to stay, and their origin can be traced in three fairly distinct forms of English legal practice. Two of these were statutory, and were the focus of the great litigations of the 1760's with which the names of Otis and Wilkes are linked. The third is the common-law warrant to search for stolen goods, which was the source of most of the procedural safeguards, against the abusive use of warrants, with which we are familiar today.

How ancient these common-law search warrants may be, we do not surely know; justices of the peace were created by statute in the fourteenth century, but apparently did not begin to issue arrest warrants until the sixteenth century.[15] Certainly the search warrant practice was well established by the middle of the seventeenth century, for it is carefully described in Sir Matthew Hale's *Pleas of the Crown*.[16] A hybrid criminal-civil process, the practice allowed the victim of theft to make oath, before a justice of the peace, of probable cause to believe that his goods would be found in such-and-such a place, where-upon the justice would issue a warrant authorizing the victim to go with a constable to the specified place and, if the goods were found, to return the goods and the suspected felon before the justice, for decision and disposition of the matter.[17]

Statutory searches and warrants are at least as old as the common-law variety. As early as 1335, innkeepers in English port cities were authorized to search their guests for counterfeit moneys.[18] During the fifteenth century, Parliament authorized several of the organized trades (for example, dyers and tallow-chandlers) to search out and destroy goods that did not meet trade standards. Licensing of books and restrictions on printing, which accompanied the oppressive laws of Elizabethan and Stuart times against sedition, led to a Star Chamber decree of 1566 which conferred on the Stationers' Company very broad powers of search, seizure, and arrest.

The agents of the Stationers' Company carried a written authority much like a warrant, and as the Star Chamber and Court of High Commission intensified their efforts to stamp out seditious libel, warrants to their "messengers" to search for incriminating documents grew ever more general and oppressive. These tribunals were abolished under Cromwell, but soon after the Restoration Parliament enacted the Licensing Act for regulation of the press, which conferred on crown officers equally broad search authority.[19] The Act expired in 1695, but despite the lack of statutory authority the Secretaries of State, as crown officers, continued to issue general warrants of search in seditious libel cases. Until the accession of George III in 1760 these warrants somehow escaped serious challenge.[20] Soon thereafter, however, the writings of John Wilkes caused the Secretary of State to issue a general search and arrest warrant which was sharply contested by several of his victims, and there ensued the first and only major litigation in the English courts in the field of search and seizure.

You will have noticed that the stream of practice I have just traced began in 1335 from a statutory source, and continued after 1695 on a common-law footing, soon to be declared defective. You may also note that the warrants, which began to be used as authority for these searches during the latter part of the sixteenth century, were issued in support of the crown's executive arm and, indeed, after the Restoration were issued by crown officers rather than judges.

The third source of our search warrants begins and remains a statutory matter, and appears to date back no further than the seventeenth century. It peculiarly concerns the revenue and customs laws, and the earliest example of which I am aware is an Order in Council of 1621 authorizing the Lord Treasurer to issue "Warrants of Assistance" for searches for unlawfully imported tobacco.[21] Parliamentary enactments of 1660 and 1662 [22] authorized the issuance of "writs of assistance" by the Court of Exchequer, for the seizure of any "prohibited or uncustomed" goods, to effect which the constables could break and enter houses, shops, and any "other Place." It was under the authority of the 1662 statute that the writs of assistance were issued which were the subject of the great case before the Superior Court of Judicature of the

Province of Massachusetts Bay in 1761. In its course James Otis made the famous argument denouncing these writs which, according to John Adams, "breathed into this nation the breath of life." [23]

You will have noticed that this triple ancestry is far from homogeneous. The old common-law warrant for stolen goods was a purely judicial device for the relief of the wronged and apprehension of the wrongdoer, with elaborate safeguards against its improvident or abusive use, and provision for immediate confrontation of the alleged miscreant and his accuser before the magistrate; well might Sir Matthew Hale observe [24] that "these warrants are judicial acts." The statutory warrants and writs of assistance were issued in aid of the crown's executive powers, and ordinarily by executive rather than judicial authority.[25] These differences may be enlightening as we examine the subsequent development of the law of search and seizure, following the accession of George III in 1760.

History of Warrantless Searches

The use of written warrants of authority, needless to say, is quite impracticable unless there are a reasonable number of officials who can read and write. Accordingly, it is hardly surprising either that the earliest statutes authorizing searches say nothing of warrants, or that it is difficult to determine with exactitude when the written document came into common or required use.

Nor, surely, would warrants be used where such a requirement would cause such delay as might frustrate the entire undertaking. From the earliest times there were both arrest and search of suspected felons, with no thought of a warrant, and it is from this natural if often oppressive practice that much of the modern law of search and seizure has sprung.

There is little reason to doubt that search of an arrestee's person and premises is as old as the institution of arrest itself. That there are very few traces of the matter in the early records is as true as it is natural, given a practice which was taken for granted, and under which suspected felons were the only victims. To be a suspected felon was often as good as being a dead one; as described by Pollock and Maitland: [26]

> The law of arrest is rough and rude; it is as yet unpolished by the friction of nice cases. . . . There is no professional police force. . . . We may strongly suspect . . . that in general the only persons whom it is safe to arrest are felons, and that a man leaves himself open to an action . . . if he takes as a felon one who has done no felony. . . . This may be one of the reasons why, as any eyre roll will show, arrests were rarely made except where there was hot pursuit after a "hand-having" thief.

Those were simple times, and felons were ordinarily those who had done violence or stolen property. Whether the chase was in hot pursuit, by hue and cry, or by a constable armed with an arrest warrant, the object was the person of the felon, and the weapon he had used or the goods he had stolen. A seventeenth-century work on the function of constables gives a broad description of the power of search incident to an arrest.[27]

> . . . For it is the chief part of their office to represse fellony, and albeit it be a man's house he doth dwell in, which

28

they doe suspect the fellon to be in, yet they may enter in there to search; and if the owner of the house, upon request, will not open his dores, it seems the officer may break open the dores upon him to come in to search. And so also it seems the officer may search for goods stoln, as he may for the Fellon himself that doth steal them; and if the Officer, upon search, cannot finde the Fellon, it is his duty to raise a Hue & Cry. . . . & upon the Hue & Cry any man may arrest him that is taken with the things (be he never so honest) & he may deliver him & the goods to the Constable of the Town to be kept safely.

Neither in the reported cases nor the legal literature is there any indication that search of the person of an arrestee, or the premises in which he was taken, was ever challenged in England until the end of the nineteenth century. When the power was then belatedly contested, as we shall see, the English courts gave the point short shrift.[28] That the practice had the full approval of bench and bar, in the time of George III when Camden and Mansfield wrote, and when our Constitution was adopted, seems entirely clear.

The Wilkes and Entick Cases: London, 1763–65

In 1762 the famous polemicist John Wilkes, a member of Parliament, began publication of a series of anonymous pamphlets entitled the *North Briton*. They were highly critical of the government's policies, including particularly the very unpopular excise tax on cider, enacted in 1763, with extensive powers of search in aid of enforcement. Following a speech by George III in which the cider excise was defended, Wilkes published the forty-fifth *North Briton*, and attacked the speech and the excise so sharply that the government decided to arrest the perpetrators and prosecute them for seditious libel. The Secretary of State, Lord Halifax,[29] issued a warrant to four messengers, authorizing search for the printers and publishers of *The North Briton*, No. 45 of April 23, 1763, and directing them to arrest any such persons, seize their papers and bring them before Halifax, to face charges of seditious libel.

The messengers cast their nets far and wide, arrested more than two-score on suspicion, and seized quantities of private papers. Some of those taken up had no connection with the *North Briton*, and several of the victims proved to be very prickly characters, who soon retaliated by suing the messengers. Opponents of the government gave the plaintiffs strong support, and it was their good fortune that their suits were heard before an unusually libertarian jurist, Charles Pratt, the Lord Chief Justice of the Court of Common Pleas.

The messengers defended their actions as authorized by the Halifax warrant. The legal issue thus tendered was the validity of the warrants of the second type that I have just described—executive warrants, originally statutory, but since the expiration of the Licensing Act in 1695 justifiable, if at all, only on the ground of long-established practice.[30] Apart from the lack of statutory authority, the warrant was totally lacking in specificity with respect to the places to be searched and the identity of the persons who, with their papers, were to be seized.

In suits by various printers who had been taken up, and later released when it appeared that they had not printed Number 45, Lord Pratt overruled the defendants' justification under the warrant,[31] and the juries returned heavy verdicts for the plaintiffs. Sitting with Lord Bathhurst on a petition by defense counsel to set aside one of the verdicts as excessive, Pratt acknowledged that the actual damage to the particular plaintiff was slight, but surmised that the jury might have looked at the liberty of the subject as a "great point," and approved the award of exemplary damages.[32]

Wilkes himself now sued one Robert Wood, an aide to Lord Halifax who had supervised the messengers while they ransacked Wilkes' home. This case, too, was tried before Pratt. Halifax testified in person that he had issued the warrant, and the Solicitor General urged that it was justified by long practice. Pratt brushed the argument aside; the precedents were unsatisfactory, the Secretary had no such powers. As for the warrant, it was hopelessly defective. No offenders' names were specified; no inventory had been made of the things taken away; the broad discretion given to the messengers was "totally subversive of the liberty of the subject." The jury returned a verdict for Wilkes to the tune of £1000.[33]

The messengers now took exceptions to the verdicts returned before Pratt, and the case came up before the Court of King's Bench in 1765, and was heard by the Chief Justice, Lord Mansfield, and Justices Wilmot, Yates and Aston.

Lord Mansfield was a mixture of politician and jurist,[34] and by no means as adventurous a magistrate as Pratt.[35] His court affirmed the judgments against the messengers, but on the narrow ground that Dryden Leach, the principal plaintiff, had not in fact printed the infamous

Number 45, and that therefore the warrant could not justify the trespass: [36] "For here, the warrant was to take up the author, printer, or publisher; but they took up a person who was neither author, printer nor publisher. . . . That makes an end of the case. . . ."

In the course of argument, however, Mansfield and his colleagues plainly enough gave it as their opinion that the Halifax warrant was invalid because too "general," in that no person was named or described in it. To be sure, "the common law, in many cases, gives authority to arrest without warrant"; likewise, "there are many cases where particular acts of parliament have given authority to apprehend, under general warrants." But here there was no statutory authority; the case must therefore "stand upon principles of common law"; on that footing "Hale and all others hold such an uncertain warrant void and there is no case or book to the contrary." Justices Wilmot, Yates, and Aston were all "clear and unanimous in opinion, that this warrant was illegal and bad." [37]

A few weeks later there came before Pratt (now Lord Camden) the last and most important of this group of cases, *Entick* v. *Carrington*.[38] In 1762 Halifax had issued a warrant for arrest of the person and seizure of the books and papers of John Entick, "the author, or one concerned in writing of several weekly very seditious papers, intitled the Monitor, or British Freeholder. . . ." Entick was arrested and his papers seized, and after his release he sued the messengers in trespass. The jury returned a special verdict of £300, and the case was laid over for argument before Lord Camden and the Court of Common Pleas *en banc.*

A large part of Camden's famous opinion was directed to the question whether the Secretary of State had the power of arrest and search, and on this point he yielded grudgingly to the affirmative answer of earlier cases. The case itself he disposed of favorably to the plaintiff on the ground that, assuming validity of the warrant, the messengers were bound to obey it meticulously, whereas they had departed from its terms by failing to take a constable with them and by bringing Entick and his papers before Halifax's assistant instead of Halifax himself.[39] Thus the jury's special verdict for Entick stood.

Unlike Mansfield, however, Camden was not content to leave the matter on so narrow a footing. He went on to discuss the validity of the Halifax warrant—a point he described as "not the most difficult" but surely "the most interesting question in the cause," because if such a warrant were held valid, "the secret cabinets and bureaus of every subject in this Kingdom will be thrown open to the search and inspection of a messenger, whenever the secretary of state shall think fit to charge, or even to suspect, a person to be the author, printer, or publisher of a seditious libel." [40]

The warrant in question was directed against Entick by name, and therefore was not deficient in the respect which Mansfield and his colleagues had found offensive in the Wilkes cases.[41] But the Entick warrant was found wanting in two basic particulars: (1) the statutory authority to search for libellous papers had expired with the demise of the Licensing Act in 1696, and (2) in any event, the warrant did not authorize merely the seizure of Entick's libellous papers, but of all of them, libellous or not.

Furthermore, the warrant had other flaws: no oath of probable cause had been given, and no record was made of what had been seized.[42]

Camden, like Mansfield, brushed aside arguments in support of the warrant based on the Secretary's past practice. The defense attempted an analogy to the common-law warrant for stolen goods, but the argument boomeranged, as Camden pointed to the judicial safeguards against abuse of the stolen goods warrant which were notably lacking in the Secretary's practice. As for the argument of state necessity,[43]

> I answer, if the legislature be of that opinion, they will revive the Licensing Act. But if they have not done that, I conceive they are not of that opinion. And with respect to the argument of state necessity, or a distinction that has been aimed at between state offences and others, the common law does not understand that kind of reasoning, nor do our books take notice of any such distinctions.

At once meticulous and sweeping, it was an opinion such as Brandeis might wish to have written. Especially telling, perhaps, was Camden's reminder that members of Parliament might themselves be the victims of such visitations, since "both Houses of Parliament have resolved, that there is no privilege in the case of a seditious libel." [44] In fact, the House of Commons had already been concerning itself with the abuse of warrants, largely at the instigation of William Pitt. On April 22, 1766 the House resolved that "a General Warrant to apprehend the author, printer, or publisher of a libel, is illegal," and that its execution on a member of the House would be a

34

breach of privilege. Three days later the House adopted a broader resolution to the effect—[45]

That a General Warrant for seizing and apprehending any person or persons being illegal, except in cases provided for by act of parliament, is, if executed upon a member of this House, a breach of the privilege of this House.

The Writs of Assistance Cases: Boston, 1761

In the colonies, it was not seditious libel but the revenue laws which led to the great controversy over writs of assistance. In describing the three principal sources of search warrants, I have already remarked on those to search for uncustomed goods, authorized by the Parliamentary enactments of 1660 and 1662.[46] The first of these was particular, requiring that oath be made that specific goods would be found in such-and-such a place. But the 1662 statute quite clearly provided for general warrants, authorizing the bearer to enter any house or other place to search for and seize "prohibited and uncustomed" goods. Furthermore, a subsequent statute (1702)[47] provided that these "writs of assistance," as they were called, should remain in force throughout the life of the sovereign and for six months thereafter.

In 1696, Parliament authorized the customs officials in the American colonies to exercise "the same powers and authorities" as those of like officials in England.[48] In most of the colonies no writs of assistance were issued, but in Massachusetts and New Hampshire the English practice was introduced. The Massachusetts Superior Court issued a general writ to the Surveyor of the Port of Boston in

1755, and English enforcement of the revenue laws tightened with the outbreak of the Seven Years' War in 1756.

George II died in October 1760, with the consequence that the 1755 writ, and others subsequently issued to other revenue officers, would expire in 1761. The Superior Court was to convene in Boston in February of that year, and with this sitting in prospect, two petitions were addressed to it. The first was by sixty-three Boston merchants—Wheelwright, Holmes, Scollay, Boylston, Lowell, Dexter and others with names redolent of the old Hub—who prayed to be heard "by themselves and Council upon the subject of Writs of Assistance." The second was by Thomas Lechmere, Surveyor General of His Majesty's Customs; it took note of the merchants' petition, and prayed "that Council may be heard on his Majesty's behalf on the same subject: And that Writs of Assistance may be granted to him and his officers, as usual." [49]

The argument for issuance of the writs, presented by the Attorney General, Jeremiah Gridley, was simple and direct. By the statute of 1662 Parliament had authorized the Court of Exchequer to issue "writs of assistance," and both the language of the act and practice under it showed them to be general writs; by the statute of 1696 the colonial customs officials had the powers of their English brethren; by provincial law the Superior Court had the jurisdiction of the English Courts of Exchequer, Common Pleas, and King's Bench; *ergo* the writs should issue.

Much of the argument for the merchants, by James Otis and his colleague Oxenbridge Thacher, is remote from the questions of the evening.[50] Highly relevant, however, was Otis' attack on the general writ as "against the fundamental principles of law." Like Camden, he contrasted it unfavorably with the common-law warrant for stolen goods, pointing out that it was both unlimited geographically and perpetual temporally, so that there was no return of the warrant before the issuing magistrate. Then, warming to his subject: [51]

> Now one of the most essential branches of English liberty, is the freedom of one's house. A man's house is his castle; and while he is quiet, he is as well guarded as a prince in his castle. This writ, if it should be declared legal, would totally annihilate this privilege. Custom house officers may enter our houses when they please—we are commanded to permit their entry—their menial servants may enter—may break locks, bars and everything in their way—and whether they break through malice or revenge, no man, no court can inquire—bare suspicion without oath is sufficient. . . . Again these writs are NOT RETURNED. Writs in their nature are temporary things; when the purposes for which they are issued are answered, they exist no more; but these monsters in law live forever, no one can be called to account. Thus reason and the constitution are both against this writ.

Mansfield and Camden had voided the Halifax writs for lack of statutory authority. The weakness in Otis' position was that the 1662 statute plainly authorized the general writs for uncustomed goods. Consequently, Otis had to fall back on the argument, drawn from Coke, that the 1662 statute itself was void as "against the Constitution" and "against natural Equity." [52] The day of parliamentary supremacy had dawned, and it was a bold contention, unlikely to persuade the provincial court. Chief Justice Thomas Hutchinson and his three colleagues suspended judgment and made inquiry to England concerning the current practice of the Court of Exchequer. Informed that general writs were commonly granted there, the Superior Court convened for reargument in November 1761, and then unanimously decided that the writs should be granted, as indeed they soon were.[53]

In most of the other colonies, writs were not sought or, if sought were refused.[54] In Massachusetts, enforcement of the writs provoked increasingly violent opposition. Hutchinson's house was burnt by a mob during the Stamp Act riots of 1765, and there was more turbulence in 1768 when John Hancock's sloop was seized under a writ. Small wonder, then, that warrants and writs were in the forefront of the colonial mind when the libertarian provisions of the early constitutions were drafted.

The Fourth Amendment: Original Understanding

If we are to seek the "original understanding" of those who framed and adopted the fourth amendment to the Constitution, it is to the foregoing materials that we should turn. The writs of assistance were anathema in the colonies, and Otis' argument against them was well known among the founding fathers. The common law was their heritage, and they vibrated in sympathy with the new libertarian trends in England. Colonial lawyers would naturally turn to the speeches of Pitt and the opinions of Mansfield and Camden—especially of the latter, whose pro-colonial speeches had won him high place in the hearts of American patriots—for eloquent exposition of English liberties, and weighty examination of the common law of searches and warrants.[55]

What, then, do we learn from these great cases of the

38

early 1760's? Of many lessons there are two, I believe, of major import to our inquiry.

In the first place, it is as plain as plain can be that these litigations involved searches under the authority of warrants, and that none of the parties was at all concerned about warrantless searches incident to arrest. The stream of practice for the latter flowed from an independent source, wholly unbroken by the rocks of controversy or litigation.

Herein there is nothing surprising, for arrest searches involved none of the abuses against which Otis and Camden railed. The only victims of such searches were those who, as probable felons, were the objects of hue and cry, hot pursuit, or an arrest warrant. Why should not their persons be subject to search for the fruits of their crimes, or the weapons, clothes or other objects that might identify them as felons in fact? If cornered in a habitation, why should not the premises be subject to a like examination? Here was no threat to the honest householder, no fear of arrogant "messengers" breaking open desks or trunks to search for smuggled jewels or libellous documents. What need for a warrant to justify a search that was so natural a concomitant of apprehending and convicting a dangerous cutthroat?

There is no evidence that suggests that the framers of the search provisions of the federal and early state constitutions had in mind warrantless searches incident to arrest. If there was any "original understanding" on this point, it was that such searches were quite normal and, in the language of the fourth amendment, "reasonable."

The other telling lesson of this history is that it was

the common-law warrant for stolen goods that embodied the requisites of "reasonable" search. The Otis and Wilkes litigations each involved one of the other two principal types of search warrants, both of which were statutory in origin, and neither of which was subject to the restrictions and safeguards that the common law had thrown around the stolen goods warrants. It is both striking and enlightening that independently,[56] in London and Boston, the opponents of the warrants based their attack primarily on unfavorable comparisons with the stolen goods warrants.

Thus Mansfield did not question, and Camden questioned but did not reject, the Secretary of State's power to commit for seditious libel and to issue arrest and search warrants in aid of that power; rather, both found fault with the style of the particular warrant. Both were critical of the warrant in the *Wilkes* cases because it was not directed to any named individual.[57] In both the *Wilkes* and *Entick* cases, Camden complained that the messengers made no inventory of what they had seized.[58] In these two respects, the Halifax warrants differed from stolen goods warrants, and in the *Entick* case Camden delivered himself of a long lecture on these and other respects in which the Halifax warrant fell short of the common-law practice, mentioning *inter alia* the lack of preliminary oath to support the search, the unsupported nature of the search, and the sweeping, indiscriminate scope of the seizure.[59]

Otis, to be sure, attacked the Superior Court's authority to issue any warrant at all, but he also laid great stress on the generality of the warrant requested. Since it was to be a warrant of indefinite duration, good until after the demise of the sovereign, Otis and Thacher especially singled out its failure to require a return of its execution before the issuing magistrate, and cited a decision of Lord Holt's [60] to show that the return was an essential feature of the stolen goods warrant: "The Writ of Assistance is not returnable. If such seizure were brot before your Honours, youd often find a wanton exercise of their Power." [61]

To summarize, our constitutional fathers were not concerned about warrantless searches, but about overreaching warrants. It is perhaps too much to say that they feared the warrant more than the search, but it is plain enough that the warrant was the prime object of their concern. Far from looking at the warrant as a protection against unreasonable searches, they saw it as an authority for unreasonable and oppressive searches, and sought to confine its issuance and execution in line with the stringent requirements applicable to common-law warrants for stolen goods—an interesting use of a practice already obsolescent to limit and mitigate a current and dangerous practice.

The language of the early constitutions amply bears out these conclusions. Between June of 1776 and July of 1777 five states—Virginia, Pennsylvania, Maryland, North Carolina, and Vermont—adopted constitutions containing "bills" or "declarations" of rights which included a provision on searches and seizures.[62] In all of them the warrant is treated as an enemy, not a friend. The Virginia clause, earliest and simplest and soon copied in North Carolina, merely condemned "general warrants" issued without supporting evidence or against unnamed persons, and the Maryland provision, though differently phrased, was substantively comparable. The Pennsylvania language, copied in Vermont, comprised a declaration that people have a "right" to be free from search and seizure, and that *therefore* warrants issued without a foundation in oath or affirmation "ought not to be granted."

It was in the Massachusetts Constitution of 1780, however, that the ancestry of the fourth amendment is most clearly to be descried: [63]

Every subject has a right to be secure from all unreasonable searches and seizures of his person, his house, his papers and his possessions. All warrants, therefore, are contrary to this right, if the cause or foundation of them be not previously supported by oath or affirmation, and if the order in the warrant to a civil officer, to make search in suspected places, or to arrest one or more suspected persons, or to seize their property, be not accompanied with a special designation of the person or objects of search, arrest, or seizure; and no warrant ought to be issued, but in cases, and with the formalities prescribed by the laws.

Except for the addition of the final clause, the probable purpose of which was to negate any official claim based on past practice rather than statutory authority, the substance of the Massachusetts clause is identical with that of the fourth amendment. Interestingly enough, as originally drafted by Madison and reported to the House of Representatives, the Amendment (like the Virginia provision) was only a prohibition of general warrants, for it recited that the "right" of the people to be "secure . . . against unreasonable searches and seizures" should "not be violated by warrants issuing without reasonable cause . . . ," etc. Under this language the general warrant would have been the specification of an unreasonable search, whereas the phrasing ultimately adopted made the warrant clause substantively independent of the initial prohibition of "unreasonable" seizures.[64] This reinforces the conclusion that it was the warrant which was the initial and primary object of the amendment.

It should now be easy to relieve the bewilderment of our distinguished colleagues who cannot understand why the fourth amendment did not prohibit as unreasonable all searches not covered by warrants issued in compliance with the second clause.[65] The framers did not do this because their prime purpose was to prohibit the oppressive use of warrants, and they were not at all concerned about searches without warrants. They took for granted that arrested persons could be searched without a search warrant, and nothing gave them cause for worry about warrantless searches.

Nothing in the legislative or other history of the fourth amendment sheds much light on the purpose of the first clause. Quite possibly it was to cover shortcomings in warrants other than those specified in the second clause; quite possibly it was to cover other unforeseeable contingencies. However that may be, the basic "original understanding" is plain enough, and might well be stated in this wise: "The power to search, seize and arrest must be kept within reasonable bounds. Warrants have been used to authorize dangerous and oppressive arrests and searches, and therefore we will now confine their issuance in line with specified requirements, developed for the

43

common-law stolen-goods warrants with which we are all familiar and which have never given any trouble." [66]

Search Warrants and Arrest Searches under the Constitution

For about a century following the adoption of the Constitution, the theory and practice of search and seizure underwent comparatively little change. The common-law warrant for stolen goods was freely utilized well into the nineteenth century, and in many states was given a statutory base.[67] Other state legislation was pretty much confined to familiar uses of warrants—to seize disease-infected or adulterated goods, or dangerous substances such as gun powder.[68] Congressional authority for federal search warrants, throughout the nineteenth century, was confined to enforcement of the revenue laws,[69] with the exception of a few special enactments dealing with obscene literature, counterfeiting of money and trademarks, and lottery tickets in the District of Columbia.[70]

Most of the court decisions during the nineteenth century relate to stolen goods warrants, and the requirements for their valid issuance and execution. Commonly these are trespass suits by the searcher against the informant or the constable; [71] occasionally the issue arises in a different context as in a criminal prosecution for assaulting the constable,[72] or a proceeding, comparable to the 1761 writs of assistance case, on the issuance of the warrant.[73] Rarely do the cases move the courts to expound a general constitutional theory of search and seizure,[74] though one finds occasional comments to the effect that provisions like the fourth amendment were intended to conform the purposes of and procedures governing search warrants in

44

accordance with the common law at the time the Constitution was adopted.[75]

There is no indication or suggestion, in any of the early statutory or case material, that the fourth amendment (or comparable state provisions) affected the power of search incident to arrest.[76] As it was before the constitutions, so was it after; the arrest search was taken for granted as needing neither warrant nor specific statutory authority.[77] The reason for the paucity of judicial treatment is not far to seek; there was as yet no exclusionary rule, and arrestees were more likely than not to be guilty, and most unlikely to be in a position to sue the arresting officer in trespass. Revenue search warrants and stolen goods warrants issued on private complaint were more likely to be procedurally defective or based on false information, and the owner of the premises searched was *pro tanto* the more likely to pursue a trespass action.

Toward the end of the nineteenth century, however, signs of a great change are perceived. The exclusionary rule for unlawfully procured evidence made its appearance in Iowa in 1903,[78] and was adopted for the federal judiciary by the Supreme Court's decision in the *Weeks* case in 1914.[79] With the growth of organized police forces, private individuals rarely if ever resorted to the stolen goods warrant as a means of recovering their property. Legislative codification of criminal procedure resulted in numerous state statutes under which search warrants became a general-purpose weapon of the police in law enforcement, since these laws commonly provided that warrants might issue not only for stolen goods, but also for the fruits and instrumentalities of crime.

During the first half of this century, a number of states

followed the lead of Iowa and adopted the exclusionary rule.[80] In all these jurisdictions the arrestee for the first time had good reason to contest the validity of the search, of his person or premises, whereby the articles, possession of which branded him a criminal, fell into the hands of the police.

The result was that the federal and some state courts were confronted with a growing volume of search and seizure cases in the context of criminal prosecution, among which were many wherein the search was incident to an arrest. There was an almost complete lack of judicial precedent for resolving these cases, for reasons already indicated.[81] As good a legal scholar as Cardozo, upholding the warrantless seizure of evidence from the person of an arrestee,[82] could cite no decisions earlier than the mid-nineteenth century,[83] for the very good reason that there were none, since such searches were never previously contested.

It was not unnatural, accordingly, that the courts looked unfavorably on the unfamiliar arrest-seizure cases, as compared with those covered by a search warrant. And so the search warrant came to be looked on, for the first time, not as a dangerous authorization, but as a safeguard against oppressive searches, and the search incident to arrest encountered, for the first time, the judicial frown.

Search Incident to Arrest: A New Look

By now the reasons should be apparent for my opening observation that Justice Frankfurter, and others who have viewed the fourth amendment primarily as a requirement that searches be covered by warrants, have stood the amendment on its head. Such was not the history of the matter, such was not the original understanding, and until about 1920 warrantless searches incident to arrest gave no cause for concern and had generated practically no case law.[84]

I hope you do not think that I would have inflicted on you this long historical exegesis only in order to show up the late Justice Frankfurter, or, indeed, anyone else. On the contrary, the problem is not primarily one of historical accuracy, but rather of the practical and, I believe, harmful consequences that flow from the mistaken view. Some of these are:

1. fostering the belief that most searches are and should be covered by warrants, when in fact most of them are not and cannot be;

2. inducing the over-simplified if not erroneous notion that warranted searches are "better" than unwarranted ones;

3. exaggerating the dangers of warrantless searches incident to arrest and the practical benefits of the warrant procedure; and

4. pushing the draftsmen of reformatory search and seizure legislation toward a false conception that the cure for the evils of search and seizure is more warrants.

There is difficulty in the statistical proof of the first point, in that most law enforcement agencies have been exceedingly lax with their record-keeping in this field.

But there are a few offices where the records are full enough to be meaningful, and from these it is abundantly apparent that searches of persons and premises incident to an arrest outnumber manyfold searches covered by warrants. This is hardly surprising; most arrests are summary (*i.e.*, before indictment), are made without an arrest warrant, and take place on the street or in private premises, more or less by way of "hot pursuit." *All* persons arrested are searched when brought to the police station, if not before. Search warrants perhaps are obtained today more frequently than they were before the *Mapp* case (1961), but they remain a tool for special situations; in the office of the District Attorney for New York County, about 95 per cent of the search warrants are obtained for the purpose of seizing narcotics and arresting the possessors.[85]

Nor does it appear to me that searches incident to arrest are more susceptible to abuse than warranted searches. At the preliminary show cause hearing, the magistrate will generally rely on the police representations, since he is unlikely to have either the time or the means to go behind them. If the Supreme Court's recent holding,[86] that the identity of informers need not be disclosed on inquiry into probable cause, survives, the protective value of the search warrant hearing will be even smaller than hitherto. True, on the return to the warrant, there is opportunity to quash it and obtain the return of anything seized, but this gives no protection against the search, and is useless if nothing has been seized. In this day and age, trespass suits against the police are a very forlorn hope.[87]

Furthermore, a warrant may issue to search the premises of anyone, without any showing that the occupant is guilty of any offense whatever. A search incident to arrest, in contrast, has a built-in limitation to cases where there is reason to believe that the subject of the search is a criminal, and where that belief is confirmed either by a valid arrest warrant or by hot pursuit or other circumstances adequate to support the belief. The ambit of harm is thus significantly narrower for search incident to arrest than for warranted searches.[88]

There is no reason to anticipate any change in the relative frequency and comparative importance of warranted and warrantless searches. Arrests are bound greatly to outnumber applications for search warrants, and arrests will continue to require searches, whether at the moment of apprehension or later. Far from regarding arrest searches as an "exception" to a general requirement that a search warrant be obtained, the reality is just the reverse: searches incident to arrest are permissible, and in exceptional cases, *if authorized by warrant,*[89] searches independent of arrest may be carried out.

A common and related misconception, to which as distinguished a judge as Learned Hand fell victim, is that a search incident to an arrest can never be broader in its physical scope than a search authorized by a warrant.[90] In fact it may often, if not usually, range more widely. A search under a search warrant is for the things described in the warrant; once they are found and seized, the authority of the warrant expires, and the search so authorized must stop.[91] But a search incident to an arrest is not for specific, predesignated articles, but for whatever may be legitimately sought and seized incident to the arrest, and the search authority may thus be narrower or wider than a warranted search, depending upon the circumstances of the arrest, including particularly the nature of the crime for which the arrest is made, and upon what is deemed in law to be legitimately "incidental" to the arrest.

There is general agreement that the person of the arrestee, and his immediate environment, may be searched for fruits and instrumentalities of the crime for which he is being arrested, and for anything which he might use as a weapon with which to resist arrest. If the arrestee is jailed, it seems clear that his person may be completely searched as an incident of his incarceration. There has been disagreement about the extent to which his body may be invaded by examining the contents of his blood stream or stomach.[92]

There has been frequent disagreement about the extent to which an arrest justifies a search of the premises in which the arrest is made.[93] On this point, the answer must depend on one's conception of the purpose of an arrest search.[94] If it is limited to seizing whatever unlawfully possessed articles or dangerous weapons the arrestee may have on his person or within grabbing distance, no or very little search of the premises is warranted. If, on the other hand, evidence of the arrestee's guilt is also a legitimate subject of seizure, a more extensive search of the premises may be legitimate.

It is to this question of "evidence" as a valid object of search, with or without a search warrant, that I now turn.

The "Mere Evidence" Rule: General

The notion that a search warrant cannot be issued for the purpose of seizing evidence of crime *qua* evidence—

the so-called "mere evidence" rule—comes as a surprise to most laymen and many lawyers. We so customarily think of seized articles as used in evidence in criminal trials, and read of motions to suppress their use as evidence, that we tend to overlook the language of the statutory authorizations under which warrants issue, most of which, until recent years, have not authorized the issuance of warrants for evidentiary purposes. Furthermore, in 1921 the Supreme Court of the United States ruled, categorically and unanimously, that the Constitution prohibits the use of a search warrant "solely for the purpose of making search to secure evidence to be used . . . in a criminal or penal proceeding." [94]

The rule was originally announced in cases involving incriminating documents. But it has also been invoked with respect to evidentiary objects. Usually these have been such as to identify the accused as the guilty party; generally they are articles of wearing apparel, such as shoes that fit footprints at the scene of the crime, or garments bearing bloodstains, or of a conspicuous color or cut that eyewitnesses of the crime observed. Sometimes, the effort to exclude these things as mere evidence has succeeded,[95] but more often the courts have found a rationale to support their reception in evidence.[96]

Indeed the assiduity with which the courts have sought and found ways to avoid an exclusionary application of the rule betrays a widespread uneasiness with the rule and its consequences. This dissatisfaction has found expression among the commentators [97] and, most recently, in several state and federal court opinions in which the rationale of the rule has been condemned on both conceptual and practical grounds.[98]

The problem has significance even beyond the dimensions disclosed by this unrest, because of its implications in legislative terms. Following the *Mapp* decision (1961), at least ten states enacted statutes explicitly authorizing the issuance of search warrants in order to obtain evidence of crime; [99] if the "mere evidence" rule endures as a constitutional standard, these statutes are, in all probability, unconstitutional. Six states have enacted statutes permitting law enforcement officials, under court order, to engage in eavesdropping by mechanical or electronic devices, and in many other states it is not prohibited.[100] A large number of state statutes permit "authorized" interception of telephone communications in aid of law enforcement.[101] Federal legislation has frequently been proposed to prohibit both wire-tapping and "bugging," subject to provisions for the use of these devices in specified circumstances and subject to various safeguards. The constitutionality of these existing and proposed laws is in part dependent upon the Supreme Court's future attitude to the "mere evidence" rule.

History of the "Mere Evidence" Rule

The rule has its origin in a passage near the end of Lord Camden's opinion in the *Entick* case dealing with defense counsel's argument that the Halifax warrant should be held valid because it served as "a means of detecting offenders by discovering evidence," to which the learned judge replied: [102]

I wish some case had been shewn, where the law forceth evidence out of the owner's custody by process. . . . In the criminal law such a proceeding was never heard of; And yet

there are some crimes . . . that are more atrocious than
libelling. But our law has provided no papersearch in these
cases to help forward the conviction. . . . It is very certain,
that the law obligeth no man to accuse himself; because the
necessary means of self-accusation, falling upon the innocent as
well as the guilty, would be both cruel and unjust; and it
should seem, that search for evidence is disallowed upon the
same principle. There too the innocent would seem to be
confounded with the guilty.

If at first sight it appears that Lord Camden relied on
the privilege against self-incrimination as directly applicable, a more careful reading indicates that he was only
using it for an analogy of policy, by pointing out that
compulsory process for evidence, *like* compelled testimony, would harm the innocent as well as the guilty.
While the rationale of the passage is not crystal-clear, I
believe that Lord Camden was simply observing, in line
with the main thrust of his opinion, that neither statute
nor common law authorized the use of search warrants to
obtain evidence of crime. As we have already seen, in
this respect he was quite right.

More than a century elapsed, however, before his
thought found an echo in Mr. Justice Bradley's opinion
in the famous *Boyd* case,[103] the first Supreme Court decision in which the fourth amendment looms large—larger,
indeed, than it should have. This was a quasi-criminal
proceeding for the forfeiture of goods alleged to have
been imported in violation of the revenue laws, under an
1874 statute [104] authorizing the court to order the defendant to produce any document which might "tend to
prove any allegation made by the United States," under
penalty that the allegation be deemed confessed. Plainly,

this was a violation of the fifth amendment's prohibition of self-incrimination, as the Court unanimously concluded. Just as plainly, it was in no respect a fourth amendment case, since the statute authorized neither search nor seizure, as Mr. Justice Miller pointed out in his concurring opinion.[105] Nevertheless, Mr. Justice Bradley's opinion for the Court held the statute invalid under both the fourth and fifth amendments.[106] Furthermore, the statute was enacted to replace an earlier one which had indeed authorized search under warrant for "books and papers relating to" merchandise charged to have been imported in violation of the revenue laws,[107] and by prodigious dictum Mr. Justice Bradley declared this earlier statute unconstitutional, and disapproved lower federal court decisions in which it had been upheld.[108]

Treating the order to produce documents as if it were a search warrant, Mr. Justice Bradley drew a distinction between cases where a warrant is issued for articles to the possession of which the government (as in the revenue cases) or the owner (in stolen goods cases) is entitled, and the case in hand, wherein the books and records were subject to no possessory claim and were the legitimate property of the party against whom the order was issued.[109] He then sought the original meaning of the fourth amendment, and quite properly turned for light on the matter to the writs of assistance case in Boston and the *Wilkes* cases in England. Describing the *Entick* case as "one of the landmarks of English liberty" and its propositions as "sufficiently explanatory of what was meant by unreasonable searches and seizures," he quoted at length from Lord Camden's opinion, including the passage respecting "search for evidence." [110] Declaring that "the language of Lord Camden" embodied "the true criteria of the reasonable and 'unreasonable' character of such seizures," and remarking that where the compulsory production of evidence is concerned "the Fourth and Fifth Amendments run almost into each other" and "throw great light on each other," Mr. Justice Bradley concluded "that a compulsory production of the private books and papers of the owner . . . is compelling him to be a witness against himself, within the meaning of the Fifth Amendment to the Constitution, and is the equivalent of a search and seizure—and an unreasonable search and seizure—within the meaning of the Fourth Amendment." And so, in a case involving neither search nor seizure, was born the constitutional doctrine that "mere evidence" is not a legitimate object of search or subject of seizure. Thirty-five years later the question came again to the Supreme Court in *Gouled* v. *United States*,[111] the case regarded as the modern cornerstone of the "mere evidence" rule, and the first search and seizure case to reach the Court following enactment of the Espionage Act of 1917,[112] in which Congress for the first time authorized the issuance of federal search warrants for property: " (1) stolen or embezzled in violation of the laws of the United States; or (2) designed or intended for use or which is or has been used as the means of committing a criminal offense. . . ." [113]

In the *Gouled* case, a search warrant issued under this statute had been used to justify the seizure of papers of "evidential value" against the owner and so used in his subsequent trial for conspiracy to defraud the United

States. Relying primarily on the *Boyd* case, the Court unanimously held that such use of a warrant violated both the fourth and fifth amendments. There was, said the Court, "no special sanctity in papers, as distinguished from other forms of property, to render them immune from search and seizure," but here the government had no such interest in the papers as to satisfy the possessory-evidentiary distinction drawn in the *Boyd* case. Since the government wanted Gouled's papers "only to use . . . as evidence" against him, the search warrant violated the fourth amendment, and the use of the papers at the trial violated his fifth amendment privilege against self-incrimination.[114]

In fact the Court should not have reached the constitutional question, for the documents had been neither used nor intended for use as the means of committing crime, and therefore lay outside the ambit of statutory authority for issuance of the warrant.[115] But the decision was unanimous and Mr. Justice Clarke's opinion was categorical, and the "mere evidence" limitation on the legitimate scope of search warrants thus became a standard part of the vocabulary of the law of search and seizure.[116] But the rule has not been much honored in the observance, for in its application the Court has often been ingenious in perceiving that documents or articles of primarily evidentiary value were also instrumentalities of the crime, and thus within both the constitutional and statutory scope of the government's powers of search and seizure.[117]

Ever since the *Entick* case, it has been the rule that search warrants (other than common-law, stolen-goods warrants) must be authorized by statute, and until the statutes immediately preceding the *Boyd* case there had been none authorizing search warrants for evidence *qua* evidence. Searches incident to arrest, however, had developed entirely from common-law practice, and were therefore free from any statutory limitations on their scope. Was the "mere evidence" rule enunciated in the *Boyd* case applicable to searches incident to arrest?

When the question arose, the courts with virtual, if not total, unanimity answered it in the negative.[118] In 1914 the Supreme Court, by way of dictum, referred to: [119] ". . . the right on the part of the government, always recognized under English and American law, to search the person of the accused when legally arrested to discover and seize the fruits or evidences of crime." Nine years later, in a New York case, the defendant moved to suppress documentary evidence taken from his person at the time of his lawful arrest, and contended that an arrest could justify no broader a seizure than a search warrant. Judge Cardozo, for a unanimous court, held that searches incident to arrest were not subject to the same limitations as applied to search warrants: [120] "The books speak broadly of searching the person of the prisoner for anything 'that may be used as evidence upon the trial' . . . or for anything 'that will aid in securing the conviction.' "

Despite an occasional and seemingly accidental dictum to the contrary,[121] the Supreme Court has adhered to the view that the "mere evidence" rule does not apply to a search of *the person* pursuant to a valid arrest. Only last year the Court upheld the taking of blood for an alcoholic content test as a reasonable search and "an appropriate incident" to the petitioner's arrest on a charge of driving while intoxicated.[122] Obviously the government had no possessory claim to the arrestee's blood, and the search was purely for evidentiary purposes.

But what of the search of the premises, as distinguished from the person, of the arrestee? Whatever the permissible spatial scope of such a search, there would seem to be neither more nor less reason to apply the "mere evidence" limitation to what might legitimately be seized. Nevertheless, and without any supporting rationale, the Court's decisions have established just such a distinction. Officers making a valid arrest under the prohibition laws searched the arrestee's room and seized numerous documents of an evidentiary nature. Citing the *Entick, Boyd,* and *Gouled* cases, the Court held the documents properly subject to a motion to suppress, on the ground that their seizure violated the defendants' rights under the fourth and fifth amendments: [123]

The decisions of this court distinguish ⌈searches of one's house, office, papers or effects merely to get evidence to convict him of crime, from searches such as those made to find stolen goods for return to the owner, to take property that has been forfeited to the government, to discover property concealed to avoid payment of duties for which it is liable, and from searches made for the seizure of counterfeit coins, burglars' tools, gambling paraphernalia and illicit liquor in order to prevent the commission of a crime."⌋

Thus the standard limitations on what may be sought and seized pursuant to a federal search warrant, including the "mere evidence" restriction, were applied to a search of immediate premises pursuant to a valid arrest.[124]

And so, in consequence of Lord Camden's opinion in the *Entick* case and by dint of two decisions, in each of which the meaning of the fourth amendment was quite unnecessarily explored, the Court has arrived at the result that the amendment bars the use of search warrants for "mere evidence," and that the same limitation applies to searches of the premises where an arrest is made, but not to searches of the person of the arrestee.

A Critique of the Rule

"*Boyd* and *Gouled* offer a rationale as simple as it is sound," according to a recent study of the question: [125]

The fifth amendment forbids any form of compulsion to obtain evidence from the accused. A search warrant, commanding obedience under pain of law is a form of compulsion. Therefore, a search warrant may not issue for the *sole* purpose of forcing an accused to turn over *his* property to the government so that the latter may introduce it against him at trial. . . . *Gouled* promulgated a rule as simple to enforce as it is simple to understand: The government may, consistent with the fourth amendment, search for and seize property, even for purely evidentiary purposes, if it can assert some *other* interest in that property recognized by law; the government is constitutionally prohibited from searching for and seizing defendant's property, for whatever reason, if there is no possessory right which it can assert either on its own behalf or on behalf of the complainant.

Simple the rationale may be,[126] but in my opinion it suffers from profound conceptual and practical difficulties. The government's possessory interest does not lift the bar of the privilege against self-incrimination with respect to process against the defendant; he cannot be required by subpoena or other process to produce the goods

59

he is alleged to have stolen or smuggled or the pistol with which he is thought to have committed the murder. Why then should the possessory factor lift the bar of the privilege with regard to seizures of such articles under a search warrant?

The fact is, of course, that search warrants can and always have been used to seize articles which are incriminating and for which, therefore, a subpoena to the defendant would not issue. A search warrant does not run against an individual, but to things in places; [127] it is quasi *in rem*. Why should the things seizable by a search warrant be limited by the possessory standard, when the government's true interest is generally (though not always) an evidentiary interest? So to conclude, without other reason, is to let fiction substitute for policy.

Furthermore, the possessory theory would be equally applicable to search incident to an arrest. Yet, as we have seen, the "mere evidence" rule has never been applied to arrest searches of the person. If shoes, shirts, or other identifying garments, in which the government's interest is purely evidentiary, may be taken from an arrestee and used in evidence against him—a proposition which has never been questioned—why should such things be beyond the reach of a search warrant?

Logic apart, however, we should pay the respect of examination to Mr. Justice Bradley's argument in the *Boyd* case [128] that the "original understanding" of the fourth amendment embraced that part of Lord Camden's opinion in the *Entick* case which criticized searches for evidence. Undeniably, the fourth amendment was intended to prohibit the abuses denounced by Lord Camden (as well as by James Otis), but it is going much further to say that it accepted every point and argument in his opinion.

Furthermore, his statements about searches for evidence must be read in the context of the case he had in hand. Lord Camden was not speaking of searches incident to an arrest, and did not have ordinary law enforcement in mind. He was not even speaking of a search warrant for specified documents issued on probable cause to believe that they would constitute proof of crime. He dealt with a seizure of all of Entick's documents, in order to rummage for such evidence of criminality as they might contain. It is doubtful that he would have taken exception to a search for specified documents, and it is certain that he would have been amazed to see his opinion invoked to shield a suspect against the taking of his shoes to match them with footprints.

Whatever Lord Camden meant in this much-discussed passage, it is worth remarking that his strictures on searches for evidence—as distinguished from his condemnation of general warrants—left no mark on the law of England. For lack of an exclusionary rule, English case law in this field is sparse, but in both of the only two important post-*Entick* decisions, seizures of purely evidentiary documents were sustained.[129] The validity of the seizure was sharply attacked on other grounds, but not for the reason that evidentiary documents are beyond the proper scope of search and seizure. Both cases involved searches of premises incident to valid arrests, and in both cases the courts upheld the seizure of evidentiary documents on the basis of the state's legitimate interest in securing "material evidence" of guilt; the *Entick* case was declared inapplicable because none of its vicious features—generality of the warrant, lack of a specific charge of criminality, and seizure of all of Entick's papers instead of those only which would have been relevant to a charge—were present.[130] Statutory authorizations of search warrants remained within traditional bounds through the nineteenth century, but in 1911, in the Official Secrets Act, explicit authorization was given for the issuance of search warrants for and seizure of "anything which is evidence of an offense under this Act having been or being about to be committed," [131] and two more recent statutes contain similar provisions.[132]

Entick apart, it might perhaps be argued that, at the time the fourth amendment was adopted, statutory authorizations of search warrants were in fact restricted to contraband and other articles in which the state had a possessory interest, and that such a limitation is therefore implicit in the amendment. But one looks in vain for any suggestion of the possessory theory in pre-constitutional times or, indeed, at any time prior to the *Boyd* case, in which it was first enunciated. Nor does the specific content of the fourth amendment lend any support to this interpretation, inasmuch as particularity of language and probable cause, rather than what may be seized, are its prime concern.[133]

It seems to me that Mr. Justice Bradley's linking of the fourth and fifth amendments has been responsible for much confusion. It is true that both the fourth amendment's restriction of searches and the fifth amendment's privilege against self-incrimination are intended to protect individual privacy and security against official intrusion and coercion. But they guard against different threats. A subpoena requires the addressee to produce, and in producing to identify, the things called for, and thus involves testimonial compulsion, against which the defendant is protected by his privilege. A search warrant calls on no one except the serving officer to identify the things seized, and exerts no testimonial compulsion. However, insofar as the fourth amendment authorizes the use of state power to obtain articles of evidentiary significance, which the owner of the premises may not obstruct even though he may be incriminated by means of the seizure, the fourth and fifth amendments are at cross rather than common purposes, as Judge Weintraub has recently pointed out.[134]

In a constitutional sense, therefore, the "mere evidence" rule is both historically and analytically unsound. Is it of any practical value? According to Learned Hand: [135] "The real evil aimed at by the Fourth Amendment is the search itself, that invasion of a man's privacy which consists in rummaging about among his effects to secure evidence against him." Therefore the rule against seizing mere evidence serves a good purpose because "limitations upon the fruit to be gathered tend to limit the quest itself, and in any case it is something to be assured that only that can be taken which has been directly used in perpetrating a crime."

That is well enough as far as it goes, but it is an argument *faut de mieux*; any limitation is better than none at all. But the "mere evidence" limitation has proved as deficient in practice as it is in theory. However commendable its consequences may be when the rule is applied to

private papers, they are absurd—or so they seem to me—
when it is invoked to bar identifying articles such as
bloody shirts. Furthermore, the rule has involved the
courts in a sterile and tortured process of distinguishing
things which are merely evidentiary from those which are
instrumentalities of the crime and therefore seizable, to
the point where a respectable court, in order to justify the
use of the defendant's shoes to match a heel print, is
obliged to treat the shoes as instrumentalities, since they
"would facilitate a robber's get-away and would not at-
tract as much public attention as a robber fleeing bare-
footed from the scene of the holdup." [136] And finally, as a
result of the courts' tendency to find "instrumentality" in
strange places, the rule has not given effective protection
against documentary rummaging.[137]

It is easy to see why professional opinion has turned
against the mere evidence rule. I conclude, therefore, that
it cannot be justified as a constitutional principle,
whether we invoke either the original understanding of
the fourth amendment or a "considered consensus" with
respect to its presently permissible scope.

It does not follow that there should be no limitations
whatever on what may be seized pursuant to a search,
whether under authority of warrant or arrest. But it is
clear that a more rational and effective test of what may
or may not be seized, than the "possessory" requirement,
is badly needed.

Bluebeard's Diary

Bluebeard's wives have disappeared one after another.
Deep suspicion hangs over him, but the authorities have
as yet no shred of evidence that he is responsible for their

deaths. Then one day his latest wife, Fatima, comes upon a book which proves to be Bluebeard's diary, in which he has recorded his slaying of her predecessors, and the location in his house of the axe with which he killed them. Fatima hears Bluebeard approaching and flees. Next morning the diary is nowhere to be seen. At the first opportunity Fatima reports her observations to the police.

In the present state of the law, the police can get a search warrant for the axe, which is an instrumentality of the crime, but not for the diary, which is "mere evidence." If they go to arrest him they may search him and seize the diary if it is on his person, but may not search his house for it.

If the mere evidence rule were to be abolished, a search warrant for the diary could be issued, and Bluebeard's papers and private repositories could be ransacked in the quest. Is this a desirable result? Bluebeard is not a sympathetic figure, but as Learned Hand reminded us in Prohibition times: [138] ". . . What seems fair enough against a squalid huckster of bad liquor may take on a very different face, if used by a government determined to suppress political opposition under the guise of sedition."

If a line is to be drawn, however, it cannot be laid between documents and other articles: [139] "There is no special sanctity in papers as distinguished from other forms of property, to render them immune from search and seizure, if only they fall within the scope of the principles of the cases in which other property may be seized." Lottery tickets are documents and at the same time articles and instrumentalities of crime, if lotteries are prohibited. Bluebeard's diary, however interesting, is not an instrumentality, and is a testimonial utterance of the diarist, which a lottery ticket is not. Account books may be both instrumental and testimonial. Do these differences among documents give us any guide to a suitable line of distinction?

Any such line should be run with an eye to the values we seek to protect. So far as concerns diaries, personal letters, and other testimonial documents, there seem to me to be three primary considerations, stemming from the first and fifth amendments, as well as the fourth.

The first of these is, of course, the freedom of the written word. The *Wilkes* and *Entick* cases were precipitated by the use of search and arrest warrants, in conjunction with the laws against seditious libel, to stifle criticism of the government, as the Court reminded us in a recent case involving the issuance of a search warrant for Communist literature.[140] Where obscene literature is the object of search, the Court has imposed higher standards of particularity in the warrant than are necessary in ordinary contraband cases, in order "to avoid suppression of constitutionally protected publications."[141] The first amendment values thus noted in cases involving published literature apply even more strongly to personal "speaking documents" of the victim of the search, and abundantly justify stringent limitation, if not total prohibition, of their seizure by exercise of official authority.

The second is the privilege against self-incrimination. It is true, of course, that searches and seizures impose only the negative obligation of non-interference, and do not call upon an accused to produce or identify anything. But diaries and letters are practically self-identifying, and if seized for evidentiary purposes would most often be used against the author for the admissions found therein. This may not be exactly the same as "the use of legal process to force from the lips of the accused individual the evidence necessary to convict him," [142] but it is perilously close—so close as to give great force to Mr. Justice Bradley's observation in the *Boyd* case that [143] "we have been unable to perceive that the seizure of a man's private books and papers to be used in evidence against him is substantially different from compelling him to be a witness against himself."

The third is the value protected by the first clause of the fourth amendment itself: that is, the right to be "secure . . . against *unreasonable* searches and seizures." The question in hand transcends the procedural safeguards of particularity and probability in the second clause. To be sure, a general warrant to seize all papers of a specified category may be even more oppressive than a warrant to seize particularly designated papers, especially if the latter be found early in the search, since the former requires a search of all the papers to isolate those which are to be seized. But, where personal papers are concerned, specificity of category is no real safeguard against the most grievous intrusions on privacy, as was pointed out over two hundred years ago during the House of Commons debates on general warrants: [144]

. . . Even a particular warrant to seize seditious papers alone, without mentioning the titles of them, may prove highly detrimental, since in that case, all a man's papers must be indiscriminately examined, and such examination may bring things to light which it may not concern the

67

public to know, and which yet it may prove highly detrimental to the owner to have made public. . . .

Of course, a search for a tiny object, such as a stolen or smuggled diamond, which can be concealed among papers or in some other small recess, may involve much the same kind of ransacking search. But at least in such a case it is unnecessary to read papers and anyhow, exceptional cases apart, it is clear that documentary searches involve deeper inroads on personal security than searches for the traditional fruits and instrumentalities of crime. As Learned Hand put it: [145]

> The real evil aimed at by the Fourth Amendment is the search itself, that invasion of a man's privacy which consists in rummaging about among his effects to secure evidence against him. If the search is permitted at all, perhaps it does not make so much difference what is taken away, since the officers will ordinarily not be interested in what does not incriminate, and there can be no sound reason in protecting what does. Nevertheless, limitations upon the fruit to be gathered tend to limit the quest itself. . . .

Perhaps this overstates the point, particularly in the light of recent cases in which the police have indeed been interested in and have seized documents which were not incriminating, at least in any legitimate sense of that word.[146] But Hand's emphasis on the search is a useful reminder that personal security is the fourth amendment's declared and prime aim, and that the danger of excessive scrutiny of private papers by official eyes was sharply etched in the memories of those who framed it.

Toward a Testimonial rather than an Evidentiary Rule

With respect to the values and dangers we have rehearsed, the "mere evidence" rule is poorly calibrated. It protects Bluebeard's diary, but has proved a poor safeguard against documentary searches, and an awkward obstacle to law enforcement in the bloody shirt situations. Learned Hand's *faut de mieux* is the best that can be said for it, and carries the point that the rule should not be simply scrapped, without replacement. The recent state statutes authorizing the issuance of search warrants for evidence of crime [147] do not meet the needs of the situation. They are essentially a reaction to the *Mapp* case, and in the blanket form they have taken, would authorize the seizure of Bluebeard's diary, and Tom Paine's as well.

I suggest, therefore, that it would be highly desirable to formulate, preferably in statutory form, a new limitation on documentary searches and seizures, drawn in testimonial terms.[148] I am well aware of the drafting difficulties inherent in such a proposal, and doubt that they can be satisfactorily overcome at one bound. But it appears to me that this is the direction in which the law of search and seizure should move, in order to achieve a better adjustment between the needs of law enforcement and the safeguards of the fourth amendment and related provisions of the Bill of Rights.[149]

The principal difficulty, of course, will be so to frame the rule as to distinguish adequately those documents which are testimonial from those which should remain subject to seizure. "Operational" documents such as lottery tickets and policy slips plainly fall in the second category, particularly since they usually will be found in bulk, and search for them will therefore not require scrutiny of private papers. The same holds true for various other categories of documents which are testimonial in the sense that they may contain admissions incriminating to the author, but which are business records or other documents required by law to be kept, and are therefore not "private" in the same sense as diaries and personal correspondence.

Warrantless searches of the person incident to an arrest have been treated as exempt from the "mere evidence" rule; on this basis even a diary could be seized if found in the arrestee's pocket. Declining to extend the exemption to incidental searches of premises, Learned Hand declared that [150]

. . . it is broadly a totally different thing to search a man's pockets and use against him what they contain, from ransacking his house for everything which may incriminate him, once you have gained lawful entry, either by means of a search warrant or by his consent. The second is a practice which English-speaking people have thought intolerable for over a century and a half.

With all respect, there is no record that the English courts have ever objected to a search of premises incident to a valid arrest, or that American courts were concerned with such a distinction until after the *Boyd* case, which was decided only forty years before Judge Hand wrote those words.

So far as concerns my proposed exemption for testimonial documents, no reason appears for distinguishing between searches pursuant to a warrant, and searches, whether of the person or of premises, incident to an arrest. The considerations drawn from the first and fifth amendments apply equally in all these circumstances. There is no good reason why a diary or personal letter, otherwise immune, should be subject to seizure when found on the arrestee's person.[151]

Rules drawn in line with these suggestions would be new in the sense that they depart from some of those now in effect. But they would be old in that they are based on policies and principles discoverable in the *Entick* case and the Bill of Rights, as Judge Weintraub and Judge Haynsworth have pointed out in recent opinions touching these points.[152] It is clear that the "mere evidence" rule's life is drawing to a close, so it is none too soon for legislators and bar committees to turn their attention in these directions.

Surveillance: The Constitutional Dimension

I come now to the final branch of my subject, to which I have applied the descriptive word "surveillance." Under this title I include the kinds of conduct commonly described as "wire-tapping" and "bugging." In more general and formal terms, I mean it to cover all imaginable kinds of clandestine official monitoring of speech and action by accoustical, optical, electronic, or other devices which extend the ambit of observation beyond the range of unaided eye and ear.

Generally speaking, law enforcement authorities have the same purpose in mind in both wire-tapping and bugging: the purpose to observe future conduct of the object of surveillance—to whom I shall refer as the "scrutinee"—and, usually, to make a record of his conduct for use as evidence against him in criminal proceedings. Despite this similarity of purpose, however, wire-tapping and bugging have not stood on the same constitutional or statutory footing.

In this field, as you all know, the law takes off from the *Olmstead* case, decided in 1928.[153] The evidentiary base

71

of this federal prosecution for conspiracy to violate the national prohibition laws consisted of numerous records of telephone conversations among the conspirators, which federal agents had intercepted. The defendants invoked the fourth and fifth amendments as grounds for exclusion of the evidence, and their arguments were supported by lawyers representing the American Telephone and Telegraph Company as *amicus curiae.* Speaking for five members of the Court, Chief Justice Taft ruled that the fifth amendment was inapplicable because there was "no evidence of compulsion to induce the defendants to talk over their telephones," and that the fourth amendment likewise did not apply because (1) it applies only to searches for "material things" which could be seized, whereas in the case at hand there was and could be "no seizure" of conversations "secured by the sense of hearing and that only," and (2) the telephone wires over which the defendants spoke were not part of a "house or office," and the amendment "cannot be extended and expanded to include telephone wires reaching to the whole world." [154] The four other justices dissented, and the opinions of Justices Holmes and Brandeis have each, though for different reasons, taken a leading place in the literature of this subject.[155]

Until recently, the *Olmstead* case has been shielded from constitutional reconsideration, because Congress provided a statutory basis for the evidentiary exclusion of intercepted telephone conversations in the federal courts,[156] and unlawfully seized evidence remained constitutionally admissible in the state courts until the *Mapp* case.[157] But the decision has been more often criticized than praised, and at least six present and former members of the Court have declared themselves in favor of overruling it.[158]

Indeed, one branch of Taft's argument in the *Olmstead* case has been overruled, and squarely though by implication. In 1961 in the *Silverman* case,[159] the Court invoked the fourth amendment to exclude from evidence in a District of Columbia "bookie" case, incriminating conversations overheard by police officers who had driven a "spike" microphone into the party wall of the defendants' premises. Since the only fruits of this surveillance were the conversations, which certainly were not tangible or "material things" which could be physically "seized," the first leg of the *Olmstead* conclusion on the fourth amendment was effectively and, I believe, rightly discarded.

But what of the other leg of the argument—the conception of the fourth amendment as protecting the privacy and security of the "home," residential or occupational, but not as extending to the far-flung network of telephone lines to which the home is connected? For reasons already indicated, the question has not, since the *Olmstead* case, been squarely posed. In three bugging cases decided at ten-year intervals, none of which involved a physical trespass upon the premises of the scrutinee, the Court upheld the use of the evidence, and found the fourth amendment inapplicable.[160] Since the opposite result was reached in the *Silverman* case, where a trespass was committed by means of the spike, it might be thought that wire-tapping remains constitutionally permissible, as long as the tap is placed outside the scrutinee's premises.

On the other hand, the trespass issue in the *Silverman*

73

case was a close one, and some members of the Court were clearly reluctant to have the constitutional question turn on a technical point of property law.[161] Especially in view of the likelihood that future cases may involve bugging of public telephone booths, lavatories, and other places which are not the property of the scrutinee, it is probable that a concept such as "protected area of privacy" may replace the traditional "a man's home is his castle" approach.[162]

Does the use of a telephone fall within such a protected area? As the Court is presently constituted, I can count only two certain and two probable votes to overrule the *Olmstead* case in this aspect.[163] In the *Silverman* case the Court had a fine opportunity to discard *Olmstead in toto*, but Mr. Justice Stewart passed it up and even gave some support to the elderly but unvenerated case by distinguishing it on the ground that it had involved no trespass.[164] Subsequent decisions, as I read them,[165] do not indicate any change in the division of the Court on this issue.[166]

So far as concerns the home, office, or other private habitation it seems to me that the trespass test has a short life expectancy. It makes no sense that the validity *vel non* of surveillance should turn on the length of the spike on the microphone, or even on whether it needs any spike whatever. With the march of science, more sophisticated listening devices require no tangible penetration of the premises. Indeed, the concept of trespass itself is changing, and tort liability is being extended to intangible intrusions.[167] The fourth amendment's application should be determined by defining the area of privacy to be protected rather than by the means used to penetrate that area, though as a practical matter it might be as well to countenance surveillance against which the scrutinee can readily protect himself by closing windows and shutters.

The question remains, however, whether the telephone network should be regarded as a projection of the home or office, in the use of which we are entitled to the same privacy as attaches to non-telephonic conversation. Perhaps it is bootless to seek the original understanding on such a point, but the quest is not without interest, if one is willing to draw analogy from the mails.

In England, the post became a state monopoly at the time of the Restoration, and in 1663 a proclamation prohibited any opening of letters save by warrant of the Secretary of State. This practice was embodied in a statute in 1710 and remains the law of England today. In line with the English system, the Constitution vested plenary power over the post in the federal government. I have seen nothing to indicate that the matter of opening letters was adverted to at the time, but had anyone then inquired into the English practice, as was often done then when difficult questions of governmental power arose, he would have found the right of interception of the mails treated as an adjunct of the sovereign monopoly of its carriage.[168]

In 1878 the United States Supreme Court had occasion to consider the constitutionality of a statute excluding lottery tickets from the mails.[169] In his opinion upholding the statute, Mr. Justice Field observed *obiter* that the fourth amendment covers sealed letters "wherever they may be," and that: "Whilst in the mail, they can only be opened and examined under like warrant, issued upon similar oath or affirmation, particularly describing the thing to be seized, as is required when papers are subjected to search in one's own household." [170] He cited no authority for this proposition, but it appears since to have been accepted without question as the law of the land.[171]

In the *Olmstead* case, however, the mail case became a bone of contention between Chief Justice Taft and Mr. Justice Brandeis. The latter thought that its authority plainly extended to telephone communications: "The mail is a public service furnished by the government. The telephone is a public service furnished by its authority. There is, in essence, no difference between the sealed letter and the private telephone message. . . . The evil incident to invasion of the privacy of the telephone is far greater than that involved in tampering with the mails." [172] The Chief Justice regarded this analogy as a failure: "The Fourth Amendment may have proper application to a sealed letter in the mail because of the constitutional provision for the Postoffice Department and the relations between the Government and those who pay to secure protection of their sealed letters. . . . The United States takes no such care of telegraph or telephone messages as of mailed sealed letters." [173]

No doubt Mr. Justice Brandeis has the better of it dialectically, but I think there is much to be said for Taft's conclusion. It is quite impossible to spell out an original understanding that the mails, or any future means of general communication, were to fall within the "persons, houses, papers, and effects" protected by the fourth amendment. By current common consensus, however, sealed mail enjoys that protection. But the telephone and telegraph require the participation of company employees, strangers to the communicants, in the transmission of messages, and in such a way that the content is often open to them. By and large, the public does not regard the telephone as being as private a medium of communication as the mails.

I conclude that, if Congress were to enact a statute specifying the circumstances under which telephone and telegraph message traffic should be subject to official surveillance in aid of law enforcement, it would be difficult to justify a decision that such a law is outside the limits of legislative power under the commerce clause. I do not believe that the fourth amendment was intended or should now be construed to prohibit such legislation.

Conversations and other conduct within a private habitation, on the other hand, fall within the primary areas that the amendment was intended to protect. I now turn to a consideration of recent legislation and legislative proposals to authorize official intrusion upon those areas for purposes of surveillance in aid of law enforcement.

Court Orders for Surveillance

Legislative reaction to the problem of surveillance has been spasmodic and diverse. In the federal dimension, as we have just seen, wire-tapping is limited by statute but not, while the *Olmstead* case remains law, by the Constitution, while the situation with respect to bugging is just the opposite. During the past thirty years numerous bills dealing comprehensively with surveillance have been introduced, but none has come close to enactment.

About three-quarters of the states have laws forbidding wire-tapping, but in most of these there is some kind of exception for law enforcement officials. Seven states prohibit bugging, but six of these have made provision for such surveillance in aid of law enforcement.[174]

The history of the matter in New York State illustrates adequately the problem I am now approaching. The state civil rights law had for many years contained a provision substantially identical to the fourth amendment. In 1938, as one of the amendments adopted following the convention held that year, a provision was added to the state constitution which brought telephone and telegraph communications within its coverage, but which also provided for the issuance of "ex parte orders or warrants" for wire-tapping, upon reasonable cause to believe "that evidence of crime may be thus obtained." [175] Four years later the legislature enacted a new section of the Code of Criminal Procedure [176] which authorized the issuance, on application by the police or district attorneys, by judges of the principal courts of first instance, of *ex parte* orders for wire-tapping, on showing spelled out in accordance with the new state constitutional provision. In 1958, the statute was amended so as to embrace bugging as well as wire-tapping, and to authorize surveillance without an order for twenty-four hours when "time does not permit" a prior application to the court.[177]

It is apparent that the New York statute flies in the face of the "mere evidence" rule.[178] I have already commented adversely on the rule and remarked its probably short life expectancy, and I am inclined to agree with

78

Yale Kamisar that if such legislation were to be constitutionally attacked on this ground, the Court would probably discard the rule in favor of the statute.[179] For me, a more difficult problem would be the application to such orders of a restriction on seizures of diaries and other testimonial documents, in line with my proposal to that effect.[180]

However that may be, the "mere evidence" rule has not been regarded as an obstacle by the proponents of a court order system for surveillance. Several other states [181] have provisions comparable to the New York law, and the *ex parte* court order is a prominent and almost omnipresent feature of the many bills to regulate surveillance that have been considered in Congress.[182] Opponents of wiretapping and bugging derive considerable comfort from the requirement of a court order, and supporters of surveillance are disposed to concede the necessity of such provisions in order to give their bills any possibility of enactment.

The *ex parte* court order has thus acquired a considerable measure of acceptance as a desirable feature of surveillance legislation. It is to the constitutional validity and practical value of such orders that I propose to devote the remainder of my time.

Surveillance Orders and Search Warrants: A Comparison

It is obvious that there is a dual rationale underlying these bills and statutes authorizing surveillance pursuant to court orders. The primary objective is to bolster the constitutionality of surveillance and thus justify the ad-

mission of evidence so obtained. Since the search warrant
has an acknowledged place in law enforcement, and
search warrants are generally issued by judges, it is hoped
that an analogy, helpful to a positive constitutional diagnosis, will be drawn between search warrants and surveillance orders. A secondary object, of course, is to guard
against unnecessary and excessive or otherwise oppressive
use of surveillance devices by the police, and thus limit
the consequent intrusions on privacy as narrowly as is
possible, consonant with the needs of law enforcement.
The interposition of a "neutral" magistrate, it is hoped,
will protect the public against the over-zealous or voyeur-
istic policeman.

Now, it needs no extraordinary faculties to perceive
differences between surveillance orders and search warrants. The warrant issues for a thing in being, let it be
dagger or document; it lies for a physical thing of some
sort, and in a sense it looks to the past, inasmuch as the
thing is in existence before the warrant issues. Thus it is
possible, as the fourth amendment requires, for the warrant to describe not only the place to be searched, but
also "the persons or things to be seized."

Surveillance orders do not fit this mold. They are not
to be issued to find and seize existing physical objects, but
to observe conduct. They look to the future, since the conduct has not yet taken place. It may be possible to describe more or less accurately the "place" to be put under
surveillance, though even in this respect the language is
hardly apt for a telephone tap, but it is quite impossible
to describe at all—let alone "particularly"—the "persons
or things to be seized." Nobody is to be seized, because as

yet there is no probable cause to arrest. Nor is there any thing to seize. Rather, it is hoped that the order will enable the police to observe the scrutinee at work or play, and, by observing, damn him with evidence of criminal ⌋ conduct.

Surely these differences are more than formal. "The warrant," as Cooley put it,[183] "is not allowed to obtain evidence of an intended crime, but only after lawful evidence of an offense actually committed." As a matter of original understanding, it is plain enough that the search warrant was never intended to be an instrument of surveillance. If it is proposed that we update the fourth amendment and rewrite its provisions so as to encompass these surveillance orders, then we should first specify the major protections against official intrusion which the amendment has provided in practice, and inquire whether or not surveillance orders will preserve or destroy those values. And if that is done, I suggest, we will find that the distinctions between search warrants and surveillance orders which have previously been remarked pale into insignificance beside two other points of difference which seem to me fatal to the attempted parallel.

The first of these turns upon the circumstance that a search warrant, although initially issued *ex parte,* becomes known to the individual, whose person or premises are the field of search, as soon as the warrant is executed. Like a temporary restraining order in equity, it is issued *ex parte* in order to freeze the situation temporarily. In equity, the purpose of the freeze is to protect the plaintiff from suffering irremediable harm before the case can be adjudicated. The warrant is *ex parte* because notice to those in control of the field of search might result in removal or concealment of its object, and thus cause, in a different sense, irremediable harm. Temporary restraining order and search warrant differ in that the initial clandestinity is a necessary feature only of the latter, but they are alike in the far more basic respect that both are ancillary *ex parte* preludes to confrontation and controversy.

Indeed, by requiring that the officer executing the warrant furnish its "victim" with a receipt for or inventory of everything seized under its authority, the common law took special pains to ensure that the warrant should lose its clandestine feature immediately upon its execution, and that a record be made in aid of whatever controversy its service and execution might generate. This procedure has remained an essential feature of search warrant practice, whether by judicial or legislative provision.[184]

The second and at least equally significant feature of the search warrant, necessarily lacking in surveillance orders, is the prompt return of the warrant to the issuing magistrate. Immediately after its execution, the officer must report on what he has done and must submit to the jurisdiction of the magistrate whatever he has seized. The return of the warrant affords immediate opportunity for the person searched to appear and move to quash the warrant, to demand the return of whatever property has been seized, or otherwise to challenge the validity of the warrant or of the action taken under its authority. Like the inventory, the return of the warrant before the magistrate was an integral part of common-law search warrant practice, and remains such today.[185]

Now, it is all too apparent that neither inventory nor return is of practicable or even possible application to surveillance orders. When one is hunting fruits or evidence of a completed crime, one can grab the stuff and give the victim immediate opportunity to challenge what has been done; even if nothing is found, he can challenge the search as not based on probable cause. But a surveillance order must not only begin as an *ex parte,* clandestine process, but also remain such. Notice to the scrutinee at any time prior to completion of the surveillance would defeat the order's very purpose. It is to laugh at the notion of serving the surveillance order on the scrutinee, informing him of the evidence which it is hoped the surveillance may turn up, and giving him prompt opportunity to challenge the order before the issuing magistrate.

To be sure, legislation authorizing surveillance orders can be so drawn as to blur these distinctions. For example, the executant officials may be required to make a "return" to the issuing magistrate, informing him of the fruits of their efforts. But this is scant comfort to the scrutinee, unless (which is most unlikely) he is to be informed of the order's existence and given opportunity to contest it. Under the surveillance order statutes so far enacted or proposed, the scrutinee never learns of the existence of the order unless and until he is indicted and tried on the basis of evidence produced by the surveillance. If such statutes were made to require that the scrutinee be in every case informed of the order at the end of the period of surveillance and then given opportunity to challenge it, the fact remains that a period of clandestine surveillance of one's private doings and sayings in the home [186] is a far greater invasion of privacy than a single search, conducted in one's presence, for specified physical objects.

In assessing the constitutionality of surveillance orders, it seems to me significant that the lack of these same procedural safeguards—*i.e.*, the inventory and the return—drew critical comment in the *Entick* and writ of assistance cases. Common-law warrant procedure, said Lord Camden, would require an "exact inventory" of what was taken, and the want of this and other precautions in the Halifax warrant "is an undeniable argument against the legality of the thing." [187] So too, Oxenbridge Thacher, Otis' colleague in the writ of assistance case, complained that the writ there sought "is not returnable," and predicted that, "If such seizure were brot before your Honours, youd often find a wanton exercise of their power." Otis echoed and re-echoed the criticism: "If an officer will justify under a writ he must return it," and again ". . . there's no return, a man is accountable to no person for his doings, every man may reign secure in his petty tyranny. . . ." [188] Surely these procedures would have been regarded as essential to the constitutional validity of a warrant by the lawyers among those who drew and adopted the fourth amendment.

The attempted analogy between search warrants and surveillance orders, I suggest, simply will not wash. Nor am I disposed to doubt that such orders would have been regarded as highly "unreasonable" under the original understanding of the first clause of the fourth amendment. No such procedure was known to the law at the time the amendment was adopted. Spike microphones were then unknown, but the same logic which supports an *ex parte* order for a clandestine trespass to install a bug would equally justify an order authorizing a King's messenger to secrete himself in Wilkes' or Entick's home to overhear and report any seditious or libellous murmurings. I am sure such a thing would have been thought outrageously unlawful, and if there is a considered consensus to the contrary today, I think it is a change for the worse.[189]

Federal Court Surveillance Orders: Case and Controversy

"Recent trends to empower judges to grant or deny wire-tapping rights to a prosecutor or to approve a waiver of prosecution in order to force a witness to give self-incriminating testimony raise interesting and dubious questions," wrote the late Justice Robert H. Jackson in a posthumously published paper: [190] "A federal court can perform but one function—that of deciding litigations—and can proceed in no manner except by judicial process." The state courts, as you all know, are not subject to the restrictions on federal judicial power found in article III of the Constitution. Justice Jackson's observation is a powerful reminder that the "cases and controversies" clause of that article bears closely on the constitutional validity of surveillance orders, insofar as currently proposed congressional legislation provides for their issuance by federal courts.

The Supreme Court's delineation of the elements of "case or controversy" has not been pellucid, but over the years certain criteria have become recognizable—adverse parties, finality of adjudication, and issues suitable for judicial resolution, to mention those most frequently invoked.[191] None of them is satisfied by surveillance orders.

Here again an analogy to search warrants is often attempted, and here again analysis reveals not a parallel, but a decisive divergence.[192]

Adversity of parties does not invariably require that adverse claims be actually presented. Probate proceedings are a good example. In most cases, fortunately for all of us, wills are probated without contest, but opportunity is given for anyone who wishes to contest the will or lay claim to a portion of the estate to appear and have his cause adjudicated. In the federal area, naturalization proceedings are an equally apt case in point, and indeed the governing rule is to be found in Mr. Justice Brandeis' opinion upholding the constitutionality of federal court naturalization: [193] are rights, liabilities, or statuses being established in a setting wherein adverse claims may be presented and adjudicated?

For reasons already given, the search warrant meets the test; the surveillance order does not. To be sure, most search warrants are not contested, but for article III purposes that is no more significant than the circumstance that most criminal cases are disposed of by consent rather than by trial. The search under the warrant is open rather than clandestine, and on return of the warrant the person searched can move to quash it, and seek the return of his property. A case or controversy is made, the issues are appropriate for judicial determination, and a final judgment can be rendered and reviewed on appeal.[194]

Surveillance orders, at least in the form authorized by statutes now on the books and bills under consideration,[195] fall short of these requirements. Execution of the order is clandestine, and the return of the order (if any) to the issuing magistrate is unknown to the scrutinee. Only if the state subsequently moves to try him on the basis of evidence obtained under the order, will he become aware that any such order has been issued and that his premises have been penetrated by surveillance. Otherwise there will be no opportunity to challenge the order, no adversity of parties, and no formal adjudication.

In short, when a judge issues a temporary intervening order, or an arrest warrant, or a search warrant, he is starting off an adversary litigation, in the sense that the person restrained, arrested, or searched can promptly challenge the legality of what has been done and seek appropriate redress.[196] But a surveillance order merely authorizes a step in the investigation of crime. The findings that the courts make in issuing warrants are that there is probable cause to believe that X has committed a crime, and that he should be arrested for trial, or that evidence or fruits of a crime exist and will be found in such and such a place, and that they should be seized for forfeiture and used as evidence, subject to the possessor's challenge. But in issuing surveillance orders, the courts are called upon to find that X will probably do or say something incriminating, and that the only way that conduct can be observed is by clandestine surveillance of a trespassory nature. Such issues are not, in my opinion, appropriate for judicial disposition, especially since the decision whether or not to subject them to review in an adversary proceeding is entirely up to the prosecuting authorities.

The non-adversary, non-justiciable nature of surveillance orders is strikingly illustrated by a case recently decided under the New York eavesdropping statute. The scrutinee, *mirabile dictu,* discovered his own status while the wire-tapping and bugging of his office was still in process. Thereupon he filed a petition to vacate the *ex parte* order, which the lower court denied without opinion. That action was affirmed by the New York Court of Appeals; two of the judges thought that the order was not judicially reviewable in any court except on motion to suppress the use of the evidence in a criminal proceeding, and two others that the lower court was not bound to review the order, and might do so or not according to its own discretion.[197] The result is that an individual who learns that he is a scrutinee has no judicial recourse against the order and its consequences; all he can do is step outside his home when he wishes to talk about his private affairs, or else take the bugging officers into his private confidence.

To be sure, it may be possible to draw a surveillance order statute which would avoid this particular problem. But the problem is only one of many. Short of provisions for elimination of the *ex parte* character of the proceeding so that at some appropriate stage in every case the scrutinees can challenge these orders, I do not see how they can be deemed to satisfy the "case or controversy" requirements of article III of the Constitution or to fall within the permissible range of federal judicial power.

Surveillance Orders and Public Policy

The constitutional considerations to which I have drawn attention are not just lawyers' technical jargon.

88

The notion that some matters are suitable and others unsuitable for judicial resolution has deep historical roots, and has demonstrated an enduring vitality that reflects policy considerations that are as important today as they were in 1789. Article III applies only to the federal courts, but these considerations are highly relevant in assessing the wisdom of statutes, like the New York example, which utilize state court surveillance orders as the basis for eavesdropping in aid of law enforcement.

The "case-controversy" requirement of adverse parties, for example, reflects the fact that courts are not investigative agencies, and are not equipped to probe disputed factual problems under their own steam. Courts rely on the parties, and the adverse interests by which they are motivated, to produce the relevant facts and demonstrate their significance. That is why the law frowns on *ex parte* orders, and allows them only as a temporary expedient to hold matters in place until the adversary element can be established or re-established.

What proper business is it of a judge, and what experience or facilities does he have, that will enable him to decide whether or not surveillance of a particular type is warranted in a particular case? Even if the judge is a former law enforcement officer, as many are, he will be unable to probe the matter in the way that opposing lawyers would. The investigative issues do not lie within traditional judicial expertise; they are intrinsically police problems, and should be handled by the executive branch.

There is great need, I believe, for an empirical study

of the issuance of these surveillance orders in the states which have authorized them. Where, as in New York, a large number of judges may issue them, I suspect study would show that their practice varies widely—that some act *pro forma*, and others inquire more or less conscientiously.[198] Conscientious or not, I believe it would also show that very few applications for surveillance orders are rejected by the judges.

In Britain, warrants for surveillance are issued by the Secretary of State. In 1957 a Committee of Privy Councillors weighed a proposal that they "should be issued only on a sworn information before magistrates or a High Court judge," and reached a negative conclusion: [199] "If a number of magistrates or judges had the power to issue such warrants, the control of the use to which methods of interception can be put would be weaker than under the present system. It might very well prove easier in practice to obtain warrants. Moreover, it would be harder to keep and collate records."

I incline to believe that in this conclusion there is much sagacity. The ability and integrity of a district attorney or other highly-placed law officer seems to me a far better safeguard against abuse than the *ex parte* order. The authorization of the judge, I fear, is not an effective screen, and may serve as window-dressing, to relieve the law enforcement official of responsibility for a decision which should be his to make. I would prefer to concentrate rather than to diffuse responsibility, and to monitor its exercise by extensive reporting requirements, and administrative review at a high level under legislatively prescribed standards.

I am aware, of course, that the spokesmen for libertarian organizations lay great store by the participation of the judge in this process, and that the court order idea commands today a wide following. Regretfully, I conclude that it is an empty and futile device. I fear that much of the support from law enforcement circles is given out of expediency, in the expectation that court orders will not much restrict the availability of surveillance, and the awareness that authorizing legislation is more likely of passage if it includes provision for such orders. And I fear that for many libertarians, court orders are a face-saving device, which enables them to say—without sufficient reason—that an important restriction is thus laid upon a technique of which they basically disapprove. For me, however, spurious safeguards are worse than none at all.

Conclusion

Personal opinion is all very well, but the battle is the payoff. How will the Court and the Congress decide the questions I have discussed tonight?

I have already ventured to predict that the "mere evidence" rule will soon meet its end, and I think it more than possible that a testimonial document exception, not unlike the rule I have suggested, will be developed by the Court.[200] On some of my other points, however, I must admit that I am swimming against the current of opinion. Worship of the warrant is widespread, and the Court has so many times treated warrantless searches as disreputable second cousins, tolerable only under the stress of exceptional necessity, that it is probably too much to hope for a reassessment of this attitude. Say what it will, however, the Court willy-nilly must grapple with the actualities of the situation, in which the search incident to arrest will continue to loom larger than the search pursuant to warrant.

The constitutional future of surveillance orders is a far more complicated matter. In dissenting opinions, several justices—including two members of the present Court—have manifested a favorable attitude toward the adaptation of search warrant procedures to surveillance problems.[201] Of these two, however, Mr. Justice Douglas has recently and explicitly repudiated any such views, and denounced warrants authorizing wire-tapping or bugging as "no different from the general warrants the fourth amendment was intended to prohibit." [202]

Mr. Justice Brennan remains as the principal spokesman on the Court for the surveillance order solution. But there are strong indications that his views would find support elsewhere on the bench, for that portion of his dissenting opinion in the *Lopez* case [203] in which he spoke in favor of surveillance orders was quoted with apparent approval in Mr. Justice Stewart's opinion for the Court in the recent *Osborn* case, in which six other members joined.[204] The reference, however, was quite unnecessary for disposition of the *Osborn* case itself,[205] and may well have been inserted to corral a majority behind a single opinion.

Perhaps we will soon have further light on the subject, inasmuch as a case under the New York eavesdropping statute is now pending before the Court.[206] On the other hand, there are other questions in the case, which may well go off on non-constitutional grounds. So, too, President Johnson has called for new congressional action in this field, but I doubt that Congress will satisfy his wishes, since on so "hot" a subject inaction may be the most discreet political path to follow.

It is quite possible, accordingly, that we will all be able to meet here again five years from now, and renew our discussion, little the wiser.

POSTSCRIPT ON FOURTH AMENDMENT DECISIONS
PRONOUNCED BY SUPREME COURT AFTER APRIL, 1967

Shortly after these lectures were delivered, and during the remainder of the Supreme Court's then current term, the Court handed down three important decisions under the fourth amendment. A fourth was delivered in December 1967. While none of them requires any significant change in the premises on which the first lecture is based, all touch directly on the questions dealt with therein.

1. *Warden* v. *Hayden,* 387 U.S. 294 (May 29, 1967).—In this case the Court reversed the decision of the Court of Appeals for the Fourth Circuit discussed *supra* at p. 51. In hot pursuit of a robber, identified by eyewitnesses of the crime in part by a light cap and dark jacket and observed to have disappeared into a particular house, the police entered the house for the purpose of arresting the suspect. While searching the house (in the course of which the ar-

93

rest was made) the police found, in a washing machine, clothing of the type described by the eyewitnesses. At trial the clothing was received in evidence against the defendant, who was convicted. The Court of Appeals, by a divided court, held that the clothing should have been excluded under the "mere evidence" rule. The majority took cognizance of the rule's increasing unpopularity, but declared themselves bound by the *Gouled* case.

By an eight to one vote, the Supreme Court reversed the Court of Appeals, and held the clothing properly admitted in evidence. In Mr. Justice Brennan's opinion for himself and four other members, the *Gouled* case was expressly overruled and the "mere evidence" rule discarded. 387 U.S. at 300–01, 306, 308–09. Mr. Justice Black concurred in the result, and wrote nothing. Mr. Justice Fortas and the Chief Justice also concurred in the result, in an opinion by the former based upon "the 'hot pursuit' exception to the search warrant requirement," which expressed disagreement with the repudiation of the "mere evidence" rule. 387 U.S. at 310–12. Mr. Justice Douglas dissented, on the ground that the rule should be preserved and applied.

Mr. Justice Brennan's rejection of the "mere evidence" rule was based upon his conclusions that (a) the rule found no support in the language of the Fourth Amendment; (b) the "possessory" theory of the rule had been discredited and was essentially a fiction, since the state's primary interest is usually evidentiary; and (c) the rule afforded no effective protection against oppressive searches, and had spawned numerous and confusing exceptions. Mr. Justice Fortas' opinion is cloudy, and can

94

be read either on the basis that identifying garments are excepted from the "mere evidence" rule, or that the rule does not apply in cases of "hot pursuit," more or less in line with the decisions justifying the seizure of evidence from the person of an arrestee.

Inasmuch as the Court's opinion speaks for only five members of whom one (Mr. Justice Clark) has already left the bench, and three members voted to preserve the "mere evidence" rule at least in large part, one cannot say with assurance that the rule is dead beyond the possibility of resuscitation. Assuming that the principal basis of the decision survives changes in the Court, it is plain that an exclusionary rule for testimonial documents, as suggested in the text (*supra* at p. 69), is possible and even probable of development. Mr. Justice Brennan did not pick up the suggestion of such a rule thrown out below by Judge Haynsworth (*supra* at p. 71), but hospitality to the idea is indicated by his remark (387 U.S. at 302–03) that: "The items of clothing involved in this case are not 'testimonial' or 'commemorative' in nature, and their introduction therefore did not compel respondent to become a witness against himself in violation of the Fifth Amendment. *Schmerber* v. *California*, 384 U.S. 757. This case does not require that we consider whether there are items of evidential value whose very nature precludes them from being the object of a reasonable search and seizure."

2. *Camara* v. *Municipal Court*, 387 U.S. 523 (June 5, 1967).—Camara, the lessee of an apartment, refused to permit a municipal housing inspector to enter and in-

spect the premises, on the ground that the inspector had no search warrant. Refusal to grant entry to an inspector was a violation of the housing code and Camara was so charged. In his defense he invoked the fourth (*via* the fourteenth) amendment, arguing that, lacking a search warrant issued on probable cause to believe that his premises contained a violation, the entry would be illegal.

Such a contention had been made unsuccessfully in *Frank* v. *Maryland,* 359 U.S. 360 (1959), decided two years before the *Mapp* case. This decision was explicitly overruled in the *Camara* case, on the ground that the citizen's "very tangible interest in limiting the circumstances under which the sanctity of his home may be broken by official authority" fully merited fourth amendment protection, especially since discovery of a violation might lead to criminal proceedings. 387 U.S. at 530–31. Speaking for the six-member majority, Mr. Justice White invoked the "governing principle, justified by history and by current experience" that "except in certain carefully defined classes of cases, a search of private property without proper consent is 'unreasonable' unless it has been authorized by a valid search warrant." 387 U.S. at 528–29. The Court also held, however, that the warrant need not be based on probable cause to believe that the premises contained a violation. Accepting the state's claim that routine "area" inspections are essential for enforcement of the housing inspection laws, the Court declared that the probable cause requirement would be met if "reasonable legislative or administrative standards for conducting an area inspection are satisfied with respect to a particular dwelling." Factors such as "the passage of time, the nature of the building . . . or the condition of the entire area" were indicated as appropriate criteria. 387 U.S. at 538. In a companion case decided the same day, the Court made these principles equally applicable to commercial premises. *See* v. *City of Seattle,* 387 U.S. 541 (1967).

Mr. Justice Clark, joined by Justices Harlan and Stewart, dissented on the basis of the *Frank* case. He invoked the history of municipal inspection laws to show that warrants had not been and should not now be required, and predicted that the majority decision "would place an intolerable burden on the inspection service when required to secure warrants." In addition, he sharply criticized the majority's modification of the "probable cause" requirement as "entirely foreign to Fourth Amendment standards" and likely to result in a system of "paper" and "boxcar" warrants which "will be printed up in pads of a thousand or more—with space for the street number to be inserted—and issued by magistrates in broadcast fashion as a matter of course." 387 U.S. at 546–55.

Since the *Frank* case was pre-*Mapp,* the majority there decided only that, as applied to inspectorial searches, the warrant clause of the fourth amendment was not an essential element of due process. At least since *Ker* v. *California,* 374 U.S. 23 (1963), however, the fourth amendment has been fully applicable to the states, and it is a little surprising to find Mr. Justice Clark, who wrote for the Court in both the *Mapp* and *Ker* cases, so indifferent to or unaware of the changed constitutional basis as between the *Frank* and *Camara* cases; his fellow dissenters in the *Camara* case (Harlan and Stewart) had not joined in Clark's opinion for the Court in the *Mapp* case.

Especially after the *Mapp* case, it appears to me that the public may not be left substantially unprotected against inspectorial searches, as they were by the *Frank* case, and that the Court was quite right to overrule it. The statutory practice of the states, on which Justice Clark relied so heavily in his dissent, is less impressive after one is reminded that these statutes were enacted before the *Mapp* or *Ker* cases had made the fourth amendment fully applicable to the states. A building inspection most certainly involves an entry into the home which, lacking official authority, would be a trespass. Comparable statutes contemporaneous with the Constitution, such as those authorizing searches for gunpowder or infected goods, often (though not invariably) required authorization by warrant. See, *e.g.*, Mass. Acts, Sess. May-Dec. 1751, ch. VI, at 421 (diseased goods); Mass. Acts, June 20, 1799, ch. IX, at 308 (abating nuisances and "sources of filth"); Mass. Acts, Mar. 12, 1808, ch. CXXXVI, at 373 (gunpowder); N.Y. Laws, 24 Mar. 1772, ch. DCXXVIII (gunpowder) ; Pa. Sess. Laws, 28 Mar. 1787, ch. LXXXIII, at 257 (gunpowder).

But the Court's therapeutics are inferior to its diagnostics. Granted that the fourth amendment applies to inspectorial searches, does this mean that the warrant clause applies to them, or the requirement that they be not "unreasonable"? Mr. Justice White appears to take the former position (387 U.S. at 534–35), but on this footing there is good ground for Mr. Justice Clark's complaint that the warrant clause is degraded, for the language and past application of that clause require probable cause to believe that the particular place to be searched be the locus of an unlawful condition, whether that be a cache of smuggled goods, or a dangerous accumulation of gunpowder.

It appears to me that the Court has again been led astray by unthinking acceptance of the too-often repeated statement that only in exceptional situations can unwarranted searches be valid—a notion that I have been at pains to criticize in the text, *supra* at pp. 46–50. The probable cause requirement of the warrant clause is simply not applicable to modern building conditions, with large and complicated structures standing cheek by jowl and elaborate networks of water, electrical, and sewage ducts, wherein the owner may be unaware of his own violation and the inspector cannot at a glance trace the symptom to the cause, and prevention by routine inspection is a *sine qua non* of community safety.

Inspectorial searches, therefore, can much better be dealt with by requiring that they be "reasonable" within the first clause of the fourth amendment. This does not, however, mean a relaxed standard; Mr. Justice Frankfurter was, I believe, quite wrong to say that inspectorial searches "touch at most upon the periphery of the important interests safeguarded by the fourteenth amendment's protection against official intrusion." See the *Frank* case, 359 U.S. at 367. On the contrary, inspectorial searches can be a vehicle of abuse ranging from officious insensitivity to corrupt or malicious oppression.

The elements of "reasonableness" for inspectorial searches are quite different from those for other sorts. Stolen or smuggled goods and murder weapons are likely to flit if the possessor suspects that the police have tumbled to their probable whereabouts. Except in rare cases, for which special provision can be made, unsafe building conditions will stay put. Therefore, in cases where consent to the entry is not given, there is no need that the authorization be issued *ex parte,* as is the case with search warrants; the owner's protest against the search can be heard and determined before it is made.

Nor is there any reason that, at least in the first instance, the authorization need be judicial. "It is unfortunate," said Mr. Justice Clark in his dissent (387 U.S. at 548 n.1), "that the Court fails to pass on the validity of the use of administrative warrants." That is a useful reminder not only of the particular possibility, but of the general proposition that judicial opinions are a poor means of legislation. In the *Camara* case, I believe that the Court would have been better advised had it simply held the state inspections statutes unconstitutional, in that they gave the inhabitants no avenue of objection to unreasonable searches, and had left it to the legislatures to consider and enact the appropriate amendatory statutes.

3. *Berger* v. *New York,* 388 U.S. 41 (June 12, 1967).— The fifth vote necessary to limit or perhaps to overrule the *Olmstead* case came from what was to me a surprising source—Mr. Justice Clark, who wrote an opinion for the Court in which three other members concurred. A fifth member, Mr. Justice Douglas, said that he concurred in the opinion, but in fact he didn't. Of the others, Mr. Justice Stewart concurred in the result on very limited grounds, and the remaining three (Black, Harlan, and

White) dissented, in individual opinions of substantial length.

The case arose under a surveillance order issued pursuant to the New York eavesdropping statute, Section 813–a of the Code of Criminal Procedure, authorizing the installation of a "bug" in the office of one Steinman. The bug was installed, and by this means the police obtained recordings of conversations in the office between Steinman and the defendant, which were subsequently used in evidence to convict the defendant of conspiring to bribe the Chairman of the State Liquor Authority in connection with the issuance of liquor licenses for the Playboy and Tenement Clubs in New York City.

The various opinions and appendices cover eighty-nine pages, and touch on a number of fourth amendment problems: the "mere evidence" rule, the application and validity of the *Olmstead* case, the specificity requirements of the warrant clause of the amendment, the constitutional validity of surveillance orders, the probable cause requirement of that clause, the exclusionary role of the *Mapp* case, and standing to raise such issues. Although no one opinion commanded a majority, on some of these matters a majority view can readily be discerned. Because of these complexities, an issue-by-issue approach appears to be the best avenue of analysis.

"Mere evidence" rule.—The *Berger* case was briefed and argued prior to the decision in *Warden* v. *Hayden;* accordingly, the petitioner relied heavily on the *Gouled* case, while the state asked that that case be overruled. In his opinion for the Court, Justice Clark disposed of the

question in a brisk footnote (388 U.S. at 44, n.2): "This contention is disposed of in *Warden . . .* v. *Hayden . . .* adversely to petitioner's assertion here." For Justices Harlan and White, it was equally clear that the *Hayden* case was conclusive on the point, 388 U.S. at 97, n.4, and 107–08, while Justices Black and Stewart did not address themselves to the point. Mr. Justice Douglas, however, adhered to his dissent in the *Hayden* case, and condemned "any electronic surveillance that collects evidence" as unconstitutional under both the fourth and fifth amendments, 388 U.S. at 67.

It is somewhat surprising that the three silent members—the Chief Justice and Justices Brennan and Fortas—were willing to go along with Justice Clark's cavalier treatment of this point. Writing the opinion for the Court in the *Hayden* case, Mr. Justice Brennan, as we have seen, was careful to leave open the possibility of some testimonial limit on the permissible objects of seizure, 387 U.S. at 303. It is true that Berger's statements were "operational" rather than "testimonial," in line with the distinction I have suggested (*supra* at p. 69), but no one on the Court took account of the particular nature of the recorded conversations. Since both the Chief Justice and Justice Fortas disagreed with the *Hayden* case's abandonment of the "mere evidence" rule (387 U.S. at 310), they might well have said something to keep open the possibility of its partial preservation.

However that may be, the *Berger* case has made it plain that the Court will not allow any relic of the "mere evidence" rule to obstruct the constitutional validity of surveillance orders, and that since only Mr. Justice Douglas thinks otherwise, the majority view will survive extensive changes in the Court's membership.

The Olmstead *case.*—The relevant passage in Mr. Justice Clark's opinion consists of four sentences, as follows (388 U.S. at 50–51):

There the interception of Olmstead's telephone line was accomplished without entry upon his premises and was, therefore, found not to be proscribed by the Fourth Amendment. The basis of the decision was that the Constitution did not forbid the obtaining of evidence by wiretapping unless it involved actual unlawful entry into the house. Statements in the opinion that a conversation passing over a telephone wire cannot be said to come within the Fourth Amendment's enumeration of "persons, houses, papers, and effects" have been negated by our subsequent cases as hereinafter noted. They found "conversation" was within the Fourth Amendment's protections, and that the use of electronic devices to capture it was a "search" within the meaning of the Amendment, and we so hold.

According to Mr. Justice Douglas concurring, and Mr. Justice Black dissenting, the Court thereby overruled the *Olmstead* case "without expressly saying so" (388 U.S. at 64 and 80), a result which the former welcomed and the latter deplored. But are they right?

The "subsequent cases" referred to by Justice Clark, he later indicates (388 U.S. at 51–52), are the *Silverman* case (*supra* at 000) and *Wong Sun* v. *United States*, 371 U.S. 471 (1936). The latter case did not at all involve surveillance, and the passage quoted by Justice Clark (371 U.S. at 485) adds nothing to the *Silverman* case, which did indeed, as we have seen (*supra* p. 73) overrule

that part of the *Olmstead* case which held that only physical objects, and not conversations, are protected by the
fourth amendment. If that is all that Justice Clark wishes
to say, he is on sound ground, but his opinion leaves the
Olmstead case exactly where it was before—overruled in
part but not in its entirety.

But there are five words in the third sentence quoted
above—"passing over a telephone wire"—which suggest
a deeper thrust. For the other leg of Chief Justice Taft's
opinion, it will be recalled (*supra* at ooo), was that the
telephone network is not a protected area. None of the
cases cited by Justice Clark as having "negated" Taft's
"statements" involved telephone communications; therefore none of them could have overruled this aspect of the
Olmstead case by implication, and certainly none did
explicitly—rather, they rendered it verbal homage. Nor
did the *Berger* case itself involve wire-tapping. If, then,
Mr. Justice Clark meant to overrule this part of the
Olmstead case, it was done by dictum, with the invocation of cases which do not support that purpose.

In the quoted passage, Justice Clark may perhaps be
seeking to contrast "statements in the opinion" which
"have been negated," with the "basis of the decision"
that a trespassory invasion of the house is all that the
fourth amendment affects. He concurred in both the
Silverman case and *Clinton* v. *Virginia* (*supra* at p. 73 and
n.161; 365 U.S. at 513 and 377 U.S. 158) only on the
ground that a trespass was committed. Especially since the
Berger case, too, involved a trespassory entry to install the
bug, it is possible that Justice Clark was seeking to protect

the *Olmstead* case only with respect to its stress on the trespassory element.

If that was his purpose, however, it is strange that on the next page (388 U.S. at 52) he should stress the significance of the language in the *Silverman* case rejecting the local law of trespass as the test. All in all, Mr. Justice Clark's swan song is, at this point in the score, mysterious music. With his departure from the bench, it still seems to me uncertain that a majority of the Court will vote for full fourth amendment protection for telephone conversations.

Specificity requirements of the warrant clause.—The outcome of the case was determined by a five-to-four decision that the New York statute was unconstitutional on its face, because the antecedent requirements for issuance of a surveillance order lacked specificity, 388 U.S. at 55–60. The respects in which the statute falls short are stated to be its failure to require (1) particularization of the crime about to be committed, the place where the surveillance is to be carried out, or the nature of the conversations to be recorded; or (2) renewed showings of probable cause to justify an extended period of surveillance; or (3) discontinuance of the surveillance as soon as the desired recording is obtained; or (4) "some showing of special facts" to justify clandestine surveillance; or (5) a return on the order to the issuing magistrate.

Only four of the justices relied exclusively on these factors as grounds for the decision; Mr. Justice Douglas "joined" the opinion to make a majority, but it is plain that he would have held the statute unconstitutional under the "mere evidence" rule even if all of the enumerated defects had been remedied. The other four justices thought the statute constitutional, each of them saying, in substance, that the Court had ignored limiting constructions put on the statute by the New York courts, and had invalidated it under standards not to be found in the fourth amendment.

Although this was the decisive point for disposition of the case, and although the New York statute was thereby invalidated, for the future these matters are not of great significance, inasmuch as statutes and "warrants" can readily be drawn so as to meet the Court's requirements, without much affecting the surveillance process.

Probable cause.—Here Mr. Justice Stewart found the narrow ground which enabled him to concur in the result, 388 U.S. at 68–70. The affidavits presented to the magistrate who issued the eavesdropping order, the justice thought, were too conclusory and furnished no basis for evaluation. Well enough they might have been for an ordinary search warrant, but the greater intrusion involved in electronic surveillance requires a correspondingly higher standard of probable cause.

No one joined Justice Stewart on this point. The majority, finding the statute invalid on its face, said that there was no need to reach the narrower question of probable cause (388 U.S. at 55), thus blandly reversing the customary order of adjudication when constitutional and nonconstitutional questions are mixed in a single pot. Justices Harlan and White thought the showing of probable cause sufficient (38 U.S. at 100–01 and 109–11), while Mr. Justice Black ignored the point.

The Mapp *case and the Fifth Amendment.*—These questions are by now of important concern only to Justices Black and Douglas. The former adheres to his view, expressed in the *Mapp* case (367 U.S. at 661), that the fourth amendment does not require the exclusion of evidence secured in violation of its provisions, 388 U.S. at 76. In the *Mapp* case, Justice Black must have thought that the unlawful entry and seizure constituted such compulsion as to bring the privilege against self-incrimination into play, but his votes in the *Osborn* and *Berger* cases make plain that he does not regard clandestine surveillance as the equivalent of compulsion for fifth amendment purposes—a view shared by everyone on the Court except Mr. Justice Douglas.

Standing.—The bug which produced the conversations that incriminated Berger was installed not on his premises, but those of Steinman. Mr. Justice Clark said (388 U.S. at 55) that it was unnecessary to determine Berger's standing to attack the eavesdropping order, since he "clearly has standing to attack the statute, being indisputably affected by it. . . ." This test of standing was sharply criticized by Mr. Justice Harlan (388 U.S. at 90), and certainly lies uneasily in the same bed with *Dennis v. United States,* 384 U.S. 855 (1966). But Berger was present in Steinman's office when the recording was made, and both Justices Harlan and White acknowledged (388 U.S. at 103 and 107) his standing to challenge the "search," under the rule of *Jones* v. *United States*, 362 U.S. 257 (1960).

Constitutional validity of surveillance orders.—This is, of course, the sixty-four thousand dollar question. Although the New York statute was held unconstitutional, the opinions in the *Berger* case strengthen the likelihood, already observable in the *Osborn* case (*supra* at p. 92), that a statute meeting the Court's procedural criteria would survive constitutional scrutiny. Indeed, it is conceivable that Mr. Justice Douglas would be a lone dissenter.

Mr. Justice Clark's opinion manifests (388 U.S. at 60–64) his awareness of the possibility that the decision would be taken as a constitutional outlawing of surveillance, and thus a serious blow to law enforcement. He sought to guard against this by citing (388 U.S. at 63) the various cases in which the Court had upheld the use of evidence obtained by electronic or other devices, from the *Goldman* case of 1942 to the *Osborn* case of 1966, laying particular stress on the *Osborn* case wherein, as he put it, the authorization was specific with respect to the "commission of a specific offense" and limited to "precise and discriminate circumstances," and the "effective administration of justice in a federal court was at stake."

The difficulty with these cases as authority for surveillance orders for bugging is that none of them involved a clandestine entry to install the bug, and none of them except possibly the *Goldman* case involved any physical intrusion whatever. The *Goldman* case did, indeed, involve an auditory intrusion into what we would today call a protected area of privacy (an office), but it was decided in 1942, before that vocabulary became fashionable, and on the explicit basis that no physical trespass had been committed. In the *On Lee* and *Lopez* cases, the government agents who interviewed the prospective defendants wore concealed devices for recording the conversations; the recording was clandestine, but not the entry, and no trespassory element was involved.

As for the *Osborn* case, elsewhere in his opinion Mr. Justice Clark describes it (388 U.S. at 56–57) as involving "an invasion of the privacy protected by the Fourth Amendment," justified only by the authorization of the judges. But Mr. Justice Stewart, writing for the Court in the *Osborn* case, did not say that it involved any such invasion of privacy, and in fact the circumstances were substantially the same as in the *Lopez* case—to wit, a government agent, who could and did testify to his conversation with the defendant, used a recording device in order to obtain corroboration for his own testimony, 385 U.S. at 326–27. No trespass was involved, the bug produced only corroboration of evidence independently obtained, and actually the case poses only the question whether the fourth amendment protects the home or office against visitation by government agents masquerading as customers or collaborators of the homeowner in order to draw him into incriminating conversations. The Court has answered that question in the negative, not only in the *Osborn* case, but also in *Lewis* v. *United States, 385* U.S. 206, decided the same day. But however that question should be decided, it is not at all the same question as is that of the validity of surveillance orders authorizing clandestine auditory or visual monitoring of the scrutinee's home, as in the *Goldman* case, much less when the order authorizes the commission of a clandestine trespass to install the bug, as in the *Berger* case, 388 U.S. at 43, 81.

Mr. Justice Clark's political prescience was better than his legal diagnosis; the decision was promptly attacked as making surveillance practically impossible. There is little basis for this assessment, for the procedural requirements listed in the decision are readily complied with, both in the authorizing statute and the "warrant" itself. Particularizations of the anticipated crime, place, and conversations are a mere matter of draftsmanship. Refreshed showings of probable cause will at worst slightly increase the administrative load.

As shown in the text, the significant difference between search warrants and surveillance orders lies in the matter of notice to the accused, so that with the return of the warrant it can be contested and any wrongfully seized articles retrieved. Had the Court insisted on a similar requirement for surveillance orders, they would indeed have been effectively blocked. But Mr. Justice Clark said only (388 U.S. at 60) that overcoming the requirement of notice would require "some showing of special facts" to justify the secrecy and the "unconsented entry"—a nice euphemism for an otherwise tortious and possibly criminal trespass. In practice, this will mean no more than that the police will say that no other means of obtaining the evidence is known to them. Certainly I doubt that any of us will live to see a surveillance order issued with notice to the scrutinee.

Already amendatory legislation has been proposed in

New York which, as far as I can see, will satisfy the *Berger* requirements. *Proposed New York Criminal Procedure Law,* N.Y. Temporary Commission on Revision of the Penal Law and Criminal Code (1967). Likewise, Justice Shapiro of the Queens County Supreme Court has ruled that, while the *Berger* case has invalidated Section 813–a, the constitutional authorization for *ex parte* surveillance orders is self-executing, and on this theory he issued an order authorizing a non-trespassory wire-tapping order shaped so as to meet the *Berger* standards. *In re Intercepting Telephone Communications,* 36 L.W. 2295 (Nov. 7, 1967).

Since it concerns a state statute and state courts, of course the *Berger* case does not touch the article III case and controversy problem raised in the text, *supra* at pp. 85–88. Neither, for reasons pointed out elsewhere above (*supra* at p. 92 n.205), did the *Osborn* case.

4. *Katz* v. *United States,* 389 U.S. 347 (December 18, 1967). Indications in the *Osborn* and *Berger* cases that the Court was preparing to put its stamp of approval on surveillance orders were proved accurate in this case, which involved the bugging of a public telephone booth. Thereby the FBI agents overheard and recorded the defendant's end of his telephone conversations, and this evidence was received at the trial which led to his conviction for transmitting wagering information by interstate wire communication.

Writing the Court's opinion, in which all its members except Justice Black (who dissented) and Justice Marshall (who took no part) joined, Mr. Justice Stewart declared that the circumstances were such that "a duly authorized magistrate . . . could constitutionally have authorized, with appropriate safeguards, the very limited search and seizure that the Government asserts in fact took place." But the FBI agents had obtained no such authorization; therefore, the surveillance was constitutionally invalid, and the defendant's conviction was reversed. The opinion is explicit to the effect that, had the agents obtained authorization following "detached scrutiny by a neutral magistrate," the surveillance would have been constitutionally sound and its fruits admissible in evidence. In view of Mr. Justice Douglas' dissents in the *Osborn* and *Berger* cases, it is remarkable that he concurred in the *Katz* opinion without qualification.

Although this was a bugging rather than a wire-tapping case, the Court's emphasis on the privacy of telephone communications, and its explicit rejection of a trespassory test, indicate that the *Olmstead* case is now overruled *in toto*, and that the same fate has overtaken the *Goldman* case. Mr. Justice Black's dissent may well be the last judicial expression in support of the *Olmstead* rationale.

For the future, Justice Stewart's opinion is also notable for its rejection of the "constitutionally protected area" vocabulary, since "the Fourth Amendment protects people, not places." The only merit in this comment is its brevity. Of course the amendment is *for the benefit* of people, not places. But it may protect peoples' places and properties—"houses, papers, and effects," in the language of the amendment—even when people are not in them or in immediate possession of them, and it may protect people themselves—i.e., "persons"—more fully when they are in one place than in another.

In a long footnote, Mr. Justice Stewart endeavors to discount the crucial difference between surveillance orders and search warrants: lack of notice and its consequences. It is not a successful effort. He invokes *Ker* v. *California*, 374 U.S. 23, 37–41 (1963) in support of the proposition that "officers need not announce their purpose before conducting an otherwise authorized search if such an announcement would provoke the escape of the suspect or the destruction of criticial evidence." But the *Ker* case is utterly inapposite to surveillance questions, for it did not involve either a clandestine search or a warrant, but rather the right of police officers making a valid arrest to enter for that purpose without prior announcement of their purpose and authority. He likewise relies on the *Osborn* case, the inapplicability of which I have already discussed, *supra* at p. 109. Finally, he declares that the Federal Rules of Criminal Procedure do not "impose an inflexible requirement of prior notice," citing *Nordelli* v. *United States*, 24 F.2d 665 (C.C.A.9th 1928). This case did indeed hold that a copy of the warrant and a receipt for the things seized thereunder need not be served before the search is begun—surely a necessary conclusion, since a receipt for what is being taken can hardly be given until the search is completed and the things to be seized have been selected. But the case was decided on the basis that the papers were left with the person searched "as required by law," and Rule 41 (d) plainly requires that the receipt be given before the officers leave the premises. It is hard to see what bearing all this has on the validity of clandestine surveillance, and it would be hard to find a more egregious misuse of authorities in the Court's reports.

The *Katz* case was a federal prosecution, so a court order for the surveillance would presumably have been a federal court order. I say "presumably," because there is no legal bar to the issuance of warrants and orders in aid of federal law enforcement by state court judges, as was the system under the very first congressional search and seizure enactment. See 1 Stat. 43 (July 31, 1789), under which search warrants in aid of the federal customs were issued by justices of the peace. However that may be, neither Mr. Justice Stewart nor any other member of the Court adverted to the article III problem.

The Court's opinion does not say that a clandestine trespass to install a bug may be authorized by an *ex parte* surveillance order, but such is plainly the consequence of its reasoning. No doubt it is comforting to be told that one's privacy is as fully protected in a public telephone booth as it is at home. But it is less reassuring to realize that one's privacy is no better protected at home than in a public telephone booth.

Part II: Fair Trial and Free Press

Fair Trial and Free Press:

First Fruits of the Warren Report

THE MAIN TITLE ABOVE is lamentably trite, but the sub-title is not. It is my hope that the tail will wag the dog, for it would, I am sure, give small satisfaction if I were to re-hearse yet again the old problem of conflicting values—the warfare, real or supposed, between the first and sixth amendments—that has been the main theme of far too many articles and addresses of the last quarter-century. Rather, I propose to focus my remarks on what is currently being actually done or responsibly recom-mended to deal with these issues.

Last night, when the subject obliged me to spend considerable time on its historical aspects, I promised that tonight there would be much less of that sort of thing. That is an easy pledge to honor, for the constitu-tional dimension of tonight's problems is less than thirty years old, and their current phase originated only three and a half years ago, in the events immediately following President Kennedy's assassination in Dallas.

Historical Background

The general question of the relationship between the bench and the press, however, has been with us for a long time, and we cannot entirely dispense with its history.

In the federal courts, the statutory framework of our subject goes back to 1831, when Congress enacted the well-known statute,[1] still on the books,[2] which limits the summary contempt power of a federal court to "misbehavior" occurring "in its presence or so near thereto as to obstruct the administration of justice." This law effectively stripped the federal courts of the power, by then well established in English judicial practice,[3] to control press comment on judicial proceedings.[4]

The 1831 statute was not, however, the product of "trial by newspaper" in the sense of that phrase today, that is, publicity tending to influence the judgment of judges or juries and thus obstruct a fair trial. Rather it was the intemperate reaction to criticism, on the part of an elderly and ailing judge, which precipitated both the law and the impeachment proceedings in which he was acquitted by a narrow margin.[5] The 1831 statute was thus an immediate reaction to an indignation-kindling episode. Accordingly, it can hardly be regarded as a considered legislative treatment of a general problem of judicial administration, but that does not make it any the less the law today, for better or worse.

That problem, however, soon made itself apparent. A recent and, to my way of thinking, excellent report on this subject by a committee of the American Bar Association,[6] treats us to a lamentation, from a legal journal of 1846, which could well have been written a century later: [7]

Ours is the greatest newspaper reading population in the world; not a man among us fit to serve as a juror, who does not read the newspapers. Every great and startling crime is paraded in their columns, with all the minuteness of detail that an eager competitor for public favor can supply. Hence the usual question, which has now become almost a necessary form in empaneling a jury, "have you formed or expressed an opinion?" is virtually equivalent to the inquiry, "do you read the newspapers?" . . . In the case of a particularly audacious crime that has been widely discussed it is utterly impossible that any man of common intelligence, and not wholly secluded from society, should be found, who had not formed an opinion.

I am not a member of the American Bar Association, and therefore feel free to cap their little treasure of historical research with an earlier and, in my view, more valuable nugget. In recent months we have had several opportunities to observe the tribulations of judges saddled with the unenviable task of empanelling a jury in sensational criminal cases. Those judges might well yearn for easier solutions availed of by their brethren of earlier times. The case I have in mind arose in 1842, and is familiar to all students of criminal law, as it is one of two famous cases raising the question of when, if ever, it is justifiable to take human life in order to save the lives of others.[8]

In 1841 a vessel bringing Scottish and Irish immigrants to America struck an iceberg off Newfoundland and foundered. Many passengers went down with her; the others and the crew took to the boats.[9] One was overloaded and in danger of sinking in heavy seas, whereupon the mate ordered the crew members to throw overboard a number of male passengers, so as to make the boat tolerably seaworthy. After this was done, the survivors were picked up by a passing vessel, and brought to Philadelphia.

As the story became known, public indignation and pressure for a prosecution mounted. The captain and mate had already shipped out, and so the charge of manslaughter was laid against one of the crew who had participated in ejecting the passengers. Since the incident had occurred on the high seas, the indictment was brought in the federal circuit court. In those days the justices of the Supreme Court rode circuit, and the case was tried before Mr. Justice Henry Baldwin and District Judge Randall. The report of the case tells us that:

The trial of the prisoner came on upon the 13th of April, 1842, a few days before the anniversary of the calamitous events referred to. The case was replete with incidents of deep romance, and of pathetic interest. These, not being connected with the law of the case, of course do not appear in this report; but they had become known, in a general way, to the public, before the trial; and on the day assigned for the trial, at the opening of the court, several stenographers connected with the newspaper press appeared within the bar, ready to report the evidence for their expectant readers.

BALDWIN, Circuit Justice, on taking his seat, now said: "By an act of congress, passed some years since, the court has no longer the power to punish, as for contempt, the publication of testimony pending a trial before us. We have, however, the power to regulate the admissions of persons and the character of proceedings within our own bar; and, as the court perceives several persons apparently connected with the daily press, whose object, we presume, is to report the proceedings and evidence in this case, as it advances, the court takes occasion to state that no person will be allowed to come within the bar of the court for the purpose of reporting, except on condition of suspending all publication till after the trial is concluded. On compliance with this condition, and not otherwise, the court will direct that a convenient place be afforded to the reporters of the press."

The reporters expressed their acquiescence in this order of the court, and the most respectful silence, on the part of the press, prevailed during the whole trial.

The act of Congress referred to by Justice Baldwin was, of course, the statute of 1831. In the particular situation, despite the limitations of the statute, the justice found an effective means of controlling press coverage of the trial. But I think we would all agree that such an order would not today be accepted so tamely by our friends of the Fourth Estate.

The things that concerned Justice Baldwin have concerned judges and lawyers—and sometimes even newspapermen—ever since. Indeed, the expression "trial by newspaper," with which these issues have commonly been labelled, may be found at least as far back as 1892, when a worried lawyer told a Chicago audience that: [10] "It has become a question of trial by newspaper or trial by the law of the land, and trial by newspaper is trial without law." We encounter it again in 1911, in an article in which the English system of suppressing publicity by the contempt power is praised.[11] The author advocated the levying of "a few heavy fines" on offending newspapers, and quoted the late Samuel Untermeyer in support of legislation imposing criminal penalties on both journalists and prosecutors for expressing opinions on the guilt or innocence of an accused.

Vociferous as they were, these early outbursts seem to have led only to the wailing wall. The first manifestation of serious professional concern was the consequence of the trial of Bruno Hauptmann, charged with the kidnap-murder of Mr. and Mrs. Charles Lindbergh's infant son. This occurred in 1935 in the town of Flemington, New Jersey, and those who remember the press reports and photographs on that occasion will surely agree that it was a Roman holiday, as undisciplined as, and more protracted than, the recent events in Dallas.

The Flemington trial was overrun and overwhelmed by the crush of radio and newsmen. The abuses, accordingly, did not especially pertain to pre-trial matters, and might best be described as "atmospheric," and obstructive of the trial proceedings themselves. A special committee was appointed by the American Bar Association, and its recommendations were directed primarily toward ensuring orderly and dignified conditions in the courtroom and its environs.[12] In this sense, the report was anticipatory of the Supreme Court's decision last year in the case of Billy Sol Estes,[13] and I have little doubt that Hauptmann, had he been given a prison rather than a capital sentence, could obtain a new trial today.

A few years after the Hauptmann case, a sensational murder trial in Baltimore (the Tarquinio "torso murders"), and the publicity which it aroused, caused the judges of the Criminal Court of that city to issue a set of rules, which constituted one of if not the earliest judicial effort to deal with the problem on more than an *ad hoc* basis. Promulgated in April, 1939 and known as the "Tarquinio Rules," they prohibited, under penalty of contempt, the issuance by the police and all counsel involved in the case, of any statement about any confessions or admissions which an accused might have made, and the publication "of any matter which may prevent a fair trial." [14]

In the early 1950's the problem flared up again, in connection with a gaudy bit of judicial business in New York City in which a young man-about-town named Mickey Jelke was charged with living off the earnings of prostitutes. A parade of spectacular witnesses gave the press a field day, and lurid testimony caused the trial judge to clear the courtroom—a move which the appellate courts disapproved, and led to the reversal of Jelke's conviction.[15] These events stirred the New York County Lawyers Association to action, in the form of a proposed "Press-Justice Code" designed to "eliminate the conflict between constitutional press freedom and constitutional fair trial." [16] It consists of a set of admonitions directed to the press, along lines by then already too familiar to anyone who had been following these matters. The "Code" did not touch the question of how its provisions might be enforced, and was purely hortatory.

These rules and reports have been issued against the background of contemporaneous Supreme Court decisions, with most of which you must all be familiar, in which the Court, under the banner of freedom of the press, has narrowly confined, if not entirely eliminated, the contempt power of state courts in this area. The federal courts, as we have seen, were already restrained by the 1831 statute. Beginning with the *Bridges* case in 1941, the Court has four times applied the first amendment (*via* the fourteenth) to set aside state court contempt convic-

tions arising out of publications.[17] At the same time, however, the Court has shown itself increasingly sensitive to
the impact of publicity on the trial process, and has reversed a number of criminal convictions—including the
famous *Sheppard* and *Estes* cases—on grounds of prejudicial publicity, involving both the press and electronic
communications media.[18]

The Warren Report and Its Progeny

In the popular sense, the "Warren Report" has come to
mean its finding, now bitterly controversial, that Lee
Oswald was the sole agent of President Kennedy's assassination. But of course the Report concerned other
matters as well, and the tragedy was of such dimensions
as to focus national attention on the event with an inten-
sity and duration far greater than had attached to the
earlier cases I have mentioned, sensational as they were.

In a sense, the power of the press was its own undoing
at Dallas, for the extraordinary publicity mirrored the
press itself. Everyone who watched television could observe what was going on in the corridors of the Dallas
court house, and hear the information, opinion, and
speculation that the officials were handing out, and see
what happened to Oswald at the hands of Jack Ruby.

It was necessary and proper, therefore, that the Warren
Report should deal with this feature of the episode,
as it did by including a section entitled "Responsibility
of the News Media." [19] That "responsibility"—in the
sense of blame for the chaotic conditions—the Commission divided between the Dallas police department
and the press:

Fair Trial and Free Press

While appreciating the heavy and unique pressures with which the Dallas Police Department was confronted by reason of the assassination of President Kennedy, primary responsibility for having failed to control the press and to check the flow of undigested evidence to the public must be borne by the police department. It was the only agency that could have established orderly and sound operating procedures to control the multitude of newsmen gathered in the police building after the assassination.

The Commission believes, however, that a part of the responsibility for the unfortunate circumstances following the President's death must be borne by the news media. The crowd of newsmen generally failed to respond properly to the demands of the police. Frequently without permission, news representatives used police offices on the third floor, tying up facilities and interfering with normal police operations. Police efforts to preserve order and to clear passageways in the corridor were usually unsuccessful. On Friday night the reporters completely ignored [Police Chief] Curry's injunction against asking Oswald questions in the assembly room and crowding in on him. On Sunday morning, the newsmen were instructed to direct no questions at Oswald; nevertheless, several reporters shouted questions at him when he appeared in the basement.

Moreover, by constantly pursuing public officials, the news representatives placed an insistent pressure upon them to disclose information. And this pressure was not without effect, since the police attitude toward the press was affected by the desire to maintain satisfactory relations with the news representatives and to create a favorable image of themselves.

The Commission made no specific recommendations, but urged others to take action:

At the annual meeting in Washington in April 1964, the American Society of Newspaper Editors discussed the role of the press in Dallas immediately after President Kennedy's assassination. The discussion revealed the strong misgivings among the editors themselves about the role that the press had played and their desire that the press display more self-discipline and adhere to higher standards of conduct in the future. To prevent a recurrence of the unfortunate events which followed the assassination, however, more than general concern will be needed. The promulgation of a code of professional conduct governing representatives of all news media would be welcome evidence that the press had profited by the lesson of Dallas.

The burden of insuring that appropriate action is taken to establish ethical standards of conduct for the news media must also be borne, however, by State and local governments, by the bar, and ultimately by the public. The experience in Dallas during November 22–24 is a dramatic affirmation of the need for steps to bring about a proper balance between the right of the public to be kept informed and the right of the individual to a fair and impartial trial.

From this very summary account of the history of this problem, you will surely have observed that public concern with it has been very episodic. There have been cycles of interest stimulated by sensational crimes and trials, and the reaction has been agonizingly repetitive.

Of course, if a speaker on this subject is content to follow well-trodden paths, this endless repetition of familiar themes makes his task very easy. One laments the unhappy conflict between first amendment freedom of speech and sixth amendment fair trial; one casts a yearning glance toward England, where there is no such conflict and the judicial contempt power seems to do the trick; one then sees a silver lining in the clouds, in that lawyers and journalists alike are men of good will; finally happy inspiration strikes, and one proposes a joint committee of press and bar, with confidence that in a spirit of good will a splendid solution will emerge from discussion. You have now been told everything of substance in numberless speeches and articles on this subject during the past thirty years.

Fortunately the impact of Dallas and the Warren Report has been deeper and more enduring. This time there has been much more than hand-wringing by way of reaction, and it is these developments in the wake of the Warren Report on which I hope to concentrate our attention tonight. A few words about each of the principal categories into which these developments have fallen may be helpful in giving us a current and practical basis for assessing the problem and its possibilities of resolution.

First to be remarked is the reaction of trial judges, who are showing themselves increasingly alert to the dangers of excessive publicity concerning the trial itself. No doubt this is in part a consequence of the Supreme Court's observation in the *Sheppard* case that the trial judge bears primary responsibility for ensuring preservation of an orderly and dignified atmosphere and a jury protected from dangerous pressures.[20] Indeed, in the widely publicized murder trial of Richard Speck in Peoria, the trial judge's restrictions were so drastic that the *Chicago Tribune* successfully challenged them in the Supreme Court of Illinois, and obtained an order for their modification.[21]

Considerably more significant, however, are the rules, or rather principles of general application, adopted by the Supreme Court of New Jersey in November 1964, by means of which the court undertook to exert a measure of control over pre-trial proceedings. These principles were enunciated in the course of an opinion on a criminal appeal by Justice John J. Francis; it may be noted that while his admonitions extend to the police and the press, the sanctions he invokes embrace only lawyers subject to disbarment proceedings: [22]

In our view *Canons* 5 and *20* of the Canons of Professional Ethics . . . ban statements to news media by prosecutors, assistant prosecutors and their lawyer staff members, as to alleged confessions or inculpatory admissions by the accused, or to the effect that the case is "open and shut" against the defendant, and the like, or with reference to the defendant's prior criminal record, either of convictions or arrests. Such statements have the capacity to interfere with a fair trial and cannot be countenanced. With respect to prosecutors, detectives and members of local police departments who are not members of the bar, statements of the type described are an improper interference with the due administration of criminal justice and constitute conduct unbecoming a police officer. As such they warrant discipline at the hands of the proper authorities.

The ban on statements by the prosecutor and his aides applies as well to defense counsel. The right of the State to a fair trial cannot be impeded or diluted by out-of-court assertions by him to news media on the subject of his client's innocence. The courtroom is the place to settle the issue and comments before or during the trial which have the capacity to influence potential or actual jurors to the possible prejudice of the State are impermissible.

Perhaps next in importance are the internal administrative regulations that have been adopted by a number of law enforcement agencies. Under the then Attorney General Nicholas Katzenbach, the Department of Justice took the lead in April, 1965 by issuing a "Statement of

Policy," binding on its own employees, which sharply restricts the release of information about pending criminal proceedings, and expressly prohibits statements about confessions, prospective testimony, ballistic and other scientific tests, and expressions of opinion about the defendant's character.[23] Both state and federal law enforcement officials in Connecticut have taken comparable action.[24]

Internal measures of self-regulation have also made their appearance among the news agencies themselves. In Toledo, Ohio, the two daily newspapers adopted, in August, 1966, a voluntary "code" under which they undertook not to publish, "unless very special circumstances dictate otherwise," an accused's prior criminal record, information about confessions or evidence excluded from the jury, and other possibly prejudicial matters.[25] The previous year, the news department of the Columbia Broadcasting System adopted its own "guidelines" for criminal news reporting, which covered two of the same points: [26]

> There are two specific areas which can be especially prejudicial to an accused and to the state's opportunity to obtain a valid conviction: confessions and previous records. Unless there are overriding public policy considerations, henceforth we will refrain from reporting such confessions and prior records until they have been admitted in evidence at the trial. However, it will still be possible (if in the judgment of a news director it is necessary to do so) simply to declare that a confession has been reported—but to go no further and give no details.

Self-regulation has also taken cooperative form, by way of "guides" or "statements" of principles adopted by joint bar-and-press committees. Even before President Kennedy's assassination, in Massachusetts such a committee in 1963 published a "Guide for the Bar & News Media," which has been adopted by a large number of the state's newspapers and broadcasters.[27] Other such guides have been agreed in Oregon and Wyoming, and in North Carolina there is the "Bench-Bar-Press-Broadcasters Committee," which meets more or less regularly to discuss, and seek agreement upon, the issues with which we are presently concerned.[28]

Finally, and of greatest interest to us tonight, are the efforts to formulate national policy in this field which have been made by major bar and press associations. On the part of the press, there has been a short but thought-provoking report by the American Society of Newspaper Editors,[29] and a considerably longer publication by the American Newspaper Publishers Association.[30] On the part of the bar, the principal statement is the report, to which I have already made reference, by an Advisory Committee to the American Bar Association, produced under the chairmanship of Justice Paul C. Reardon of the Supreme Judicial Court of Massachusetts.[31] Also widely publicized is the report by a special committee of the Association of the Bar of the City of New York, headed by Judge Harold R. Medina, of the Court of Appeals for the Second Circuit.[32]

Three and a half years have now passed since the issuance of the Warren Report. Its main impact on this matter has been felt, and from now on it will be a diminishing stimulus to either thought or action. I have surveyed its immediate fruits,[33] and I propose now to scrutinize with some care the viewpoints and recommendations of the organized press and bar, especially those of the bar, as embodied in the ABA and ABNY reports. In doing so, I shall also take account of the Supreme Court's two most recent and pertinent decisions—the *Sheppard* and *Estes* cases—although in fact neither of them goes very far to resolve our problems, especially in the pre-trial stage of criminal process.

Major Categories of Prejudicial Publicity

I hope that it has not escaped your notice, in the review we have just made of these various rules and reports and recommendations, that there is a remarkable degree of agreement in identifying the particular kinds of publicity which may threaten the fairness of a trial. This accord is by no means confined to the legal profession; the framers of the self-imposed codes such as those adopted by the Toledo newspapers and the Columbia news broadcasters, and the press representatives who have joined in press-bar codes like the Massachusetts "guide," have all recognized precisely the same sources of danger as have the lawyers concerned with the problem.

These dangers fall into two general categories. The first is publicity by which a community, and thus the jurors and other participants in a trial, is permeated with a preconception of the defendant's guilt. This may be accomplished by denunciation or derogatory descriptions of the accused, by sensational photographs and constant emphasis on lurid details of the crime, by predictions about the evidence, and in a host of other ways by which so many people come to believe the defendant guilty that the selection of an impartial jury is rendered exceedingly difficult if not impossible. Much more rarely, such publicity may be favorable to the defendant and impose an unfair burden on the prosecution. And, at some times and places, the press may have helped to cultivate racial or other attitudes that dictate the conviction or acquittal of the defendant regardless of what the evidence shows.

The second type is publicity which informs jurors about matters which are excluded by law from their attention and consideration. These include such things as a defendant's previous criminal record, which may not be shown at the trial unless he takes the stand in his own defense, or a confession or admission which is excluded at the trial because it is found to have been the product of coercion. Had Lee Oswald been brought to trial, for example, the facts furnished by Mrs. Oswald could not have been proven by her testimony, since under Texas law a wife may not testify against her husband.[34] Yet it would surely have been difficult to find jurors who were not aware, through press or radio reports, of the information furnished the police by Mrs. Oswald.

The ABA Report contains an excellent descriptive analysis of the kinds of publicity which may be prejudicial.[35] In addition to criminal records and confessions, these include reports that an accused has declined to submit himself to tests, for example, by polygraph; results of technical tests, such as fingerprint or ballistic identifications; mention of plea-bargaining; expressions of official opinion that they "have the right man," or that witnesses will give conclusive testimony; or the disclosure to jurors of proceedings conducted while the jury was excluded from the courtroom.

Of course, the mere tabulation of these danger points does not get us far toward specific remedies, and it is not my purpose tonight to propose a code of prohibitory rules. But the record of action and discussion since the Warren Report plainly shows that our difficulty does not lie in identifying the kinds of publicity which rightly cause concern for the integrity of the judicial process.

When, however, we turn to the question of what, if anything, should be done about all this, we find ourselves fairly drowned in disagreement, not only between the press and the bar, but within the bar itself. Not only is there next to no agreement on the kind of sanctions that might be used to check these abuses; rather, we confront at the threshold of the problem a strong contention, on the part of responsible spokesmen of the press, that there is really no problem at all, or at most a very insignificant one, and that any cure is bound to be worse than the disease.

Accordingly, I will now undertake an assessment of the magnitude of the problem that confronts us, before examining the rules and remedies proposed in the ABA and ABNY reports.

Magnitude of the Problem

Far from accepting the strictures in the Warren Report, the nationally-organized press has taken a very dim view of both its criticism of press conduct in Dallas, and its recommendations for ameliorative action. I will return presently to certain other aspects of the press reaction; at the moment I want to discuss one theme which runs through many pronouncements from the organized press, including both the ASNE and the ANPA reports.

I am referring to their contention that this problem has been inflated far beyond its true magnitude. The notion that jurors are prejudiced by pre-trial publicity, they say, is an utterly unproven assertion, based on un-lawyer-like assumptions. Furthermore, it is argued, the number of criminal cases to which publicity attaches is very small, both absolutely and as a fraction of the entire criminal process. In short, say these spokesmen for the Fourth Estate, restraints are being urged to guard against a danger which is largely a figment of the overheated legal imagination.

Let us first consider the contention with respect to the influence of publicity on jurors. The suggestion is, I take it, that jurors who have previously read in the press that an accused has confessed, or that ballistic tests show that the fatal bullet was fired by his gun, may well be able to render an unprejudiced verdict, even though such evidence may not, for one reason or another, be offered or admitted at the trial. To this ef-fect, the ANPA Report tells us: [36]

Some segments of the American Bar appear to have begun their discussions of the Free Press-Fair Trial question with the assumption that pre-trial reporting of facts in criminal matters is itself prejudicial to a defendant. This is a presump-tion for which no concrete proof is advanced. There are cases cited, of course, in which it is *believed* that a defendant's rights are imperiled by "pre-trial publicity." But that is simply a conjecture—and not a fact. Indeed, in bringing such charges of prejudice in pre-trial reporting, the Bar is not only indicting but convicting without clear evidence that such is true.

And, in the same vein, according to the ASNE Report: [37]

Convincing or even credible evidence on the degree to which press coverage of criminal proceedings injures the chances of fair trials for defendants is almost totally lacking. In argument on the issue, the standard pattern has been a deriving of sweeping conclusions from the most incomplete, fragmentary and isolated sets of facts.

In the whole study of American jurisprudence, we are aware of no competent demonstration of the effect of pretrial and trial publication on the minds of jurors.

I must confess that these arguments came as a surprise to me, as I believe they do to most lawyers who have tried criminal cases to a jury. Especially when the trial is of some notoriety, or involves complex political and social issues, the effects of publicity seem apparent to any lawyer who has been through a protracted *voir dire*. Often the effects are given explicit statement in the juror's replies to question, often it can be sensed in ways that are difficult to articulate—by what the Germans call *Fingerspitzengefühl*.

But all this is far clearer to a harassed trial lawyer than to a suspicious journalist, and it is perfectly true that the extent to which jurors (or judges, for that matter) are susceptible to prejudice by publicity has been too much taken for granted by the bar. Despite the invaluable studies by Kalven and Zaisel,[38] and others, the jury room has remained a sanctum beyond the reach of direct research.[39]

The ABA Report took note of this issue, and made an effort at its illumination by means of the field study which accompanied this report. Questionnaires were sent to some 200 defense lawyers practicing in twenty large and middling cities, and their answers clearly reflected a general belief that publicity can and does have a prejudicial effect.[40]

But of course this is all opinion and impression, not specific proof. The ABA questions were loosely phrased, and the yield from the questionnaire has been subjected to trenchant criticism by Dr. Frank Stanton of the Columbia Broadcasting System, whose response is worth quoting at some length: [41]

But there is no in-depth study here, and you can look in vain for a comparison of convictions in nonpublicized cases to those in publicized cases. It is true that the Report's staff did send representatives to 20 cities to do a "content analysis" of crime reporting. But it was admitted that they could make only a "subjective judgment" as to whether "questions of potential prejudice" arose from the reporting they examined.

Such "judgments," which would be thrown out of a court of law as evidence as fast as they would be from a social scientist's laboratory, were never followed up for result statistics. We have all these sober "content analyses" and not a single instance of how much actual prejudice the news reports of "potential prejudice" produced in the end.

In the same cities, questionnaires were sent to defense counsel asking how many times they "thought" the news reports created "a significant problem of possible prejudice." Eighty-three percent of those responding indicated that they had had such a thought on one or more cases.

In addition to its tolerance for such substantive ambiguities as "thoughts" of *"possible* prejudice" (emphasis added), the

ABA Report showed startling inexactness in statistical analysis.

It is claimed, for example, that the "numerical responses" from the defense attorneys added up to 320 cases of "thoughts" of "possible" prejudicial reporting. But there were only 54 out of 200 defense attorneys—barely one out of four—who bothered to answer, and one of these thought he had 100 such cases—an advocate obviously peculiarly sensitive to the freedom of the press.

It is undeniable that presently available statistical data on this question would hardly pass muster either in a court of law or a social scientist's "laboratory," whatever such a room might amount to. Dr. Stanton is a hard man to satisfy; what he insists on is a demonstration that the rate of convictions is higher when there is supposedly prejudicial publicity than it is where such news is suppressed, as it is in England. Of course, even such a demonstration would be vulnerable to hostile analysis, as it is virtually impossible to establish adequate controls, or eliminate countervailing or contributing factors.[42]

But despite the unsatisfactory statistical basis for any firm conclusions, I cannot help feeling that much of this dispute is tactical shadow-boxing. The fact is that jurors *say* that they are prejudicially affected by pre-trial publicity, and sometimes say it in great numbers. I have been reading the newspaper accounts of the Speck murder trial proceedings, and see that it has taken over a month to impanel a jury. The four jurors unfortunate enough to have been the first ones chosen were accepted on February 22, and had to be sequestered until March 30, when the last four were finally selected. Of the

595 veniremen questioned, nearly 300 were excused because they had formed a fixed opinion that Speck was guilty.[43] One must wonder how many of those who denied having such an opinion were either sincere or sufficiently introspective.

Such cases are unusual but by no means unprecedented. The reports readily disclose comparable occasions, extending back as far as 1895.[44] In one of the cases wherein a conviction was reversed by the Supreme Court because of prejudicial publicity,[45] over 400 veniremen were called, the record on *voir dire* totalled 2,783 pages, and eight of the jurors impanelled thought the defendant guilty at the time they were chosen. More recently, the Speck and Hoffa trials have borne ample witness to the same effect. Such cases, as well as my own experience in controversial if less sensational criminal cases, seem to me a sufficient demonstration that jurors are indeed susceptible to pre-trial publicity, and that most of them are well aware of it.

But our journalistic brethren have another string to the bow. Even assuming that juror susceptibility is a fact, they say, the number of cases to which publicity of dangerous dimensions attaches is very, very small—a "pitiful little string" of cases, according to a well-known Richmond editor. Here is how the point is put in the ASNE Report: [46]

Only a small fraction of criminal cases go to jury trials in any event; one estimate puts the number at 8 per cent. Of these, a still much smaller fraction are reported by the press. Clifton Daniel, managing editor of the New York Times, noted that in January, 1965, 11,724 felonies were committed

138

in New York City and of these, only 41 were mentioned in the New York Daily News, which gives more attention to crime than any other newspaper in the city. One recent study declares that of the several hundred thousand criminal trials in the United States in the last two years, there have been only 51 cases where prejudicial pre-trial publication has been urged as a basis for a reversal of conviction, and that from these, only three actual reversals ensued.

Now, of course it is true that most criminal cases are disposed of on the pleas, and a very good thing that is, for if the situation were otherwise, we would all be so busy trying criminal cases that there would be no time for anything else. It is equally fortunate that most contract disputes are resolved without going to court, and that most fires are put out without calling the fire department. As things are, whether it is 8 or 10 per cent of criminal cases which actually go to trial, our courts are glutted, the calendar lags, and justice is far too long delayed.

Furthermore, the argument proves too much, for if we were to treat the percentage of criminal cases that go to trial as insignificant, we might as well stop worrying about the rules of evidence, or the right of confrontation, or any of the many other matters that relate to the conduct of a trial. Somewhat less than 10 per cent of all the deaths in the United States are caused by automobile and other accidents, but no one suggests that the problem of accidental death is unimportant.

Finally, trials are much more significant in the administration of criminal justice than is indicated by the mere numbers. The outcome of trials and the rules by which they are conducted furnish the pattern and base of comparison which enables the others to be settled without trial. When a criminal case is disposed of on the pleas, the trial is present in spirit, though not in flesh.

What about the point that only a few of the cases that go to trial are affected by publicity? On this score the ABA Report, in my opinion, has made a useful contribution. The underlying field study included an analysis of newspaper crime reporting in 23 cities of various size, based on categories of possibly prejudicial trial disclosures by the police or the prosecution, *e.g.,* reports of the content of confessions, the accused's refusal to take tests, official opinion of the accused's guilt, etc.[47] The study shows not only a large number of such reports, but also a wide variation among the cities, reflecting differences in official practice with respect to releasing such information. In San Francisco, for example, during the six-month period covered by the survey there were twenty-six reports of confessions in state and local crime cases; in Pittsfield, Massachusetts there were none at all. In Newark, New Jersey there were 22 such reports in a 50-day period prior to the announcement of the *Van Duyne* rules,[48] but only 7 in the six months following that decision.[49]

To summarize, it seems to me that common experience on *voir dire* and the ABA field study give us ample reason to conclude that jurors *are* prejudicially affected by publicity, and that the problem is one of substantial magnitude. At the same time we must acknowledge that there are significant aspects of jury behavior about which we know far too little, and that our understanding of the effects of publicity is sketchy. Furthermore, public acceptance of the need for ameliorative measures may well depend on a more compelling demonstration of the hazards than has yet been made. Intelligently planned research in this area, accordingly, is very much to be desired.

Sanctions

If what I have just finished saying may not sit very well with my friends in the world of news, I doubt that it will arouse much disagreement within the legal profession. But I now come to the far more difficult problem of what to do in order to cope with the problems I have described, and am thus entering an area of controversy in which the bar itself is deeply divided.

Sanctions to curb publicity may take numerous forms. They may be internal and administrative—for example, guidelines such as those formulated by the cbs news department, enforced by the employer against the employee by means of reprimand, or penalty, or even discharge. Comparable official administrative sanctions might be used in police departments or prosecutors' offices.

Such internal disciplinary measures might present, in their formulation, difficult questions of policy, but not of law. Legal questions certainly do arise, however, if we contemplate the imposition of sanctions by force of law, whether declared in the form of criminal statutes, or applied in contempt proceedings.

If criminal sanctions are to be applied directly against the press, the constitutional limits derived from the first amendment will narrowly confine their permissible scope if, indeed, any such sanctions are constitutionally valid. Countervailing constitutional values drawn from the fifth and sixth amendments may, to be sure, be invoked, but even if the constitutional hurdles might thus be surmounted there would remain the most serious issues of policy to be weighed before embarking on such a course.

The ABA Report makes it plain that the police are the most frequent source of pre-trial disclosures. Presumably they are subject to both legislative and executive regulation, and so could be subjected to either administrative or criminal sanctions prescribed by the legislature. Do the courts also have power, by contempt, to regulate police behaviour in this respect? As we shall see, the bar is in disagreement on this point, on which the ABA and ABNY reports present opposing views.

Prosecutors are government employees, and thus subject to whatever controls can be imposed on the police. Defense counsel are not, but defense and prosecution lawyers alike are "officers of the court" and subject to the discipline of the bar. Therefore the sanctions of that discipline—reprimand, suspension, and disbarment—may be available, as well as contempt proceedings and statutory restrictions.

Of course, we should not forget that there are other means of combatting the effect of publicity: change of venue, continuance, liberal rules of disqualification on *voir dire,* and sequestration of the jury are familiar devices available for this purpose. So, too, convictions tainted by prejudicial publicity can be reversed. But all these techniques are imperfect and wasteful, and in this era of mass communications media change of venue is increasingly ineffective.

Nor do I overlook the close relation between the quality of judicial administration and its suspectibility to distortion by publicity. If there are fewer confessions which are inadmissible because tainted by coercion or other factors, publicity about confessions will do *pro tanto* less harm.

In the foreseeable future, however, even if we succeed in substantially raising the over-all quality of the criminal process, the hazards of publicity will nevertheless abide with us. The question is, then, which if any of the items in this arsenal of sanctions may we constitutionally, and should we as a matter of policy, invoke. Let us examine first the attitude of the organized press, and then the bar proposals, particularly those embodied in the ABA and ABNY reports.

The Intransigent Press

As we have seen, individual press and radio-television enterprises, and local or regional news associations, have initiated or joined in voluntary guides or codes for the prevention of prejudicial publicity. On the national level, however, press reaction to the Warren Report, and to most proposals for the control of crime reporting, has been uncompromisingly hostile.

This negative reaction extends to the events in Dallas with which the Warren Report is concerned, and includes a vigorous rejection of the criticisms it voiced of press behavior in the Dallas courthouse. Listen to the words of the ANPA committee, in its report: [50]

The background from which this Committee received its charge was the release of the Warren Commission Report on the assassination of John F. Kennedy. In that report the press of America was charged with "irresponsibility and lack of self-discipline." A review of the press performance in those dark days at Dallas shows that such criticism was unwarranted. In crisis on November 22, 1963, the American press was called upon to carry out its responsibility to the people—to tell them not only what had happened, but how the country met the crisis. It was those facts provided by the American press that steadied a reeling nation and a shocked and startled world. The American Press should have been commended rather than censured for its performance.

But it was the Warren Commission Report which triggered the guns of attack on the press, and the cry that the free press is the enemy of fair trial was heard again. Our studies, our historical experience, our common sense, prove the opposite of this contention. They are not incompatible, but dependent one upon the other.

For its part, the ASNE Report uses as its point of attack the statement in the Warren report that [51] "neither the press nor the public had a right to be contemporaneously informed by the police or prosecuting authorities of the details of the evidence being accumulated against Oswald," and counters it as follows: [52]

With all respect, your committee disagrees fundamentally with this statement. It was not mere public curiosity—a word made to seem pejorative in this context—that demanded satisfaction. The matter was as essential to the citizens of a democracy as any other that can be imagined. Particularly because of the history of Oswald—and it is not pleasant to think how it would have appeared if the inescapable revelation of it had been spread only by word of mouth through a furious and grief-stricken nation—the most complete and exact information was required at once.

Merely to state the idea that there could or should have

been less than complete disclosure is to indicate its impossibility. It is worth letting the imagination run for a moment on what the consequences would have been to the persons and property of both right- and left-wing groups in the United States, to Oswald's widow, to his and her former associates, and indeed to the public attitude about relations with the Soviet Union, had any areas in the whole ghastly episode been hidden behind a curtain of official secrecy during the first 24 to 72 hours after the fatal shots. For the public to have been left speculating, guessing and ultimately inventing for the several weeks, or more probably months, before Oswald could have been brought to trial would have been a course fraught with the greatest dangers.

Now, it is undeniable that when a President is assassinated, it cannot be expected that everyone's first concern will be insuring a fair trial for the suspected killer. There are other values at stake, and national survival is a higher one. Priority must be given to ascertaining the source of the peril, and finding out whether or not the peril has passed.

These activities may indeed make it more difficult later on to impanel an unbiased jury for the trial of the accused assassin, and that is unfortunate. So far we may go with the ASNE Report, but of course that is not the full story of Dallas, where the enormous pressures of an avid press on a pliant police department resulted in the publication of a great deal of *mis*information, as well as unfounded and unnecessary expressions of opinion. These same pressures then produced the circumstances which made possible Oswald's killing by Jack Ruby, and thus caused loss of the prime source of information, Lee Oswald himself. The substance of the Warren Report's strictures, on both police and press, seems to me wholly justified.

More important for our present purposes is the unmitigated opposition of the press associations to legal sanctions of any kind. This hostile attitude is by no means confined to sanctions to be applied to the press, with respect to which strong negative arguments of law and policy can readily be advanced. But the press attitude goes to the limit of intransigence here in opposing, with almost equal fervor, sanctions or administrative restrictions applicable to the police, or to the lawyers involved in the case, whether for the prosecution or the defense. Any such provisions, designed as they are to stem the flow of prejudicial information, are denounced as "gag rules" or worse.

The basis of this opposition may be found in two different arguments, or ways of putting the same argument. The first of these is a right, ostensibly claimed by the press in behalf of the general public, which is described as the "right to know." It is presented as the last and climactic "conclusion" of the ANPA Report: [53]

The people's right to a free press which inherently embodies the right of the people to know is one of our most fundamental rights, and neither the press nor the Bar has the right to sit down and bargain it away.

I have been encountering this phrase for a long time, and it has gained nothing by repetition. It seems to me a very woolly mouthful. The verb "to know" is transitive, but as used here it is left dangling helplessly, with no object. When and to what does this right attach? Granted that there is great value in an enlightened and informed public, it does not follow that every identity or episode should be immediately publicized, whether it is the breaking of an enemy code in wartime, or the name of an adolescent rape victim in peacetime.

There is no need to belabor the point. However completely the first amendment may protect the press against restrictions on what it may print or penalties for what it has printed, even under Mr. Justice Black's absolutist view of the amendment it imposes no general obligation on officials to disclose everything to the press. Certainly it is constitutional, whether or not it be wise, to withhold information which, if disclosed, might threaten the integrity of the judicial process.

But the other argument, or the other formulation, has much more substance. It is stated in one of the other ANPA "conclusions" as follows: [54] "To fulfill its function, a free press requires not only freedom to print without prior restraint but also free and uninhibited access to information that should be public." This is question-begging, but it is buttressed by the explicit assertion: "The press is a positive influence in assuring fair trial." The point is elaborated, in a more sophisticated way, in the ASNE Report: [55]

In a community, for example, where crimes against a given race or group are traditionally tolerated, publication of the facts about the crime and the suspect may be the instrument that forces rather than obstructs justice. Much the same is true where the malefactor has friends in high places or closely aligned with the political structure of a community. And when similar forces are bent on railroading an innocent man, his protection as well as the proper ends of justice are served by publication—by news coverage that would often be impossible if the press were constrained by an arbitrary set of rules about what it could and could not publish prior to trial.

I believe this point to be entirely valid and of major significance, in both constitutional and policy terms. However, I cannot resist observing that the press does here precisely what it accuses the bar of doing in gauging the magnitude of the publicity problem, that is, indulging assumptions without adequate or, indeed, any specific proof. How often does the press make contributions of the kind described in the ASNE Report? In more than a "pitiful little string" of cases? Here is the best that the ANPA Report can do on that point: [56]

It is pertinent at this point to cite the words of the third man in the Free Press-Fair Trial discussion. That man is the defendant himself, and here are the words of a convict, Hugh Dillon, writing in the Southern Michigan prison publication. "As distasteful as adverse publicity may be," he said, "it is better to be spotlighted momentarily than abused in darkness."

That is the full extent of the field study in support of the point, and it needs no Dr. Stanton to perceive its inadequacy. On this score, the ABA has done much better for the press than the press has done for itself,[57] in pointing to instances where the press has helped to "guard against unlawful or unnecessary arrests and detentions as well as other abuses of the rights of those in custody," and in producing "evidence that either supports the prosecution or helps to establish the innocence of the person accused," as in the recent and notorious Whittemore case in New York City,[58] wherein press activity led to discrediting the confession which had been extorted from him.

Despite the lack of precise information, I think we should conclude that the value, though imponderable, is weighty, and that full opportunity for press scrutiny of the judicial process has rightly been accepted in this country as a cornerstone of the body politic. This is, in fact, the principal reason why the English practice of controlling publicity by summary contempt cannot be transplanted to our shores. The English seem to have more faith in the police and less faith in the press than we do. They pay a price, however, in that the English press is far from crusading on matters of criminal justice, and there are recent signs that the price may be too high.[59] However that may be, the viewpoint in this country is well stated by Mr. Justice Clark, in his opinion in the *Sheppard* case: [60]

A responsible press has always been regarded as the handmaiden of effective judicial administration, especially in the criminal field. Its function in this regard is documented by an impressive record of service over several centuries. The press does not simply publish information about trials but guards against the miscarriage of justice by subjecting the police, prosecutors, and judicial processes to extensive public scrutiny and criticism. This Court has, therefore, been unwilling to place any direct limitations on the freedom traditionally exercised by the news media for "[w]hat transpires in the court room is public property." *Craig* v. *Harney*, 331 U.S. 367, 374 (1947). The "unqualified prohibitions laid down by the framers were intended to give to liberty of the press

. . . the broadest scope that could be countenanced in an orderly society." *Bridges* v. *California,* 314 U.S. 252, 265 (1941). And where there was "no threat or menace to the integrity of the trial," *Craig* v. *Harney, supra,* at 377, "we have consistently required that the press have a free hand, even though we sometimes deplored its sensationalism."

But Mr. Justice Clark's praise of the benefits of publicity, it will be noted, was carefully qualified by the words quoted from the *Craig* case: "no threat or menace to the integrity of the trial." The values of publicity are not put forward as absolutes, and ensuing passages from his opinion underline the Court's concern that "the jury's verdict be based on evidence received in open court, not from outside sources." In the reports of the national press associations, I am bound to say, we find little help in dealing with the problems of judgment and balance thus posed.

I cannot escape the feeling that, with commendable but rare exceptions, the press has reacted to Dallas and the Warren Report tactically rather than on the merits. The journalists view that Report as the harbinger of restrictions, perhaps not on themselves but on their sources of information. Wishing to fend off these limitations or hold them to a minimum, the members of the Fourth Estate have concluded that the best offense is a good defense. Accordingly they put a bold face on Dallas, pooh-pooh the dimensions of the problem, and wrap themselves in the mantle of free speech, behind the shield of the first amendment. That is why the ANPA Report is more a manifesto than the "study" it purports to be, and cannot be taken seriously as a contribution to the handling of the problem.

But if weak on the merits, these arguments have been highly successful as tactics. At the bar of public opinion the journalists have been far more successful advocates than have the lawyers. We hear no talk today of contempt and heavy fines, such as was heard from Samuel Untermeyer half a century ago. With few exceptions, the members of the bar are proposing no direct restraints on the press, and their proposals of other sanctions are coupled with apologetic mumbling about "cleaning our own house." Whether this restraint is the product of tactical prudence or honest conviction is debatable. However that may be, the marks of caution are visible on every page of the two principal bar studies—the ABA and ABNY Reports—to which I now turn in conclusion.

The ABA and ABNY Reports

Both of these organizations—one the leading national and the other an unusually distinguished local association—appointed special committees, with prestigious membership, to conduct their studies. The chairman of the ABA committee was Paul Reardon, Associate Justice of the Supreme Judicial Court of Massachusetts, and of the ABNY committee, Circuit Judge Harold Medina, of the Court of Appeals for the Second Circuit. The ABA Report was based on the newspaper content analysis and the answers to questionnaires that I have already described, and the ABNY Report was preceded by a voluminous but largely unanalyzed survey of radio and television broadcasts and other materials relating to criminal justice.[61]

The two reports show, in common with other studies and codes, a broad agreement on the kinds of publicity that tend to prejudice the criminal process. But they are far apart in their recommendations for dealing with these abuses, in that the ABNY Report proposes no sanctions other than revision and enforcement of an existing canon of professional ethics, whereas the ABA proposals embrace important though limited resort both to the contempt power and to legislative prohibitions and sanctions.

In recommending the amendment and increased use of Canon 20 of the Canons of Professional Ethics, the ABA and ABNY reports are on common ground.[62] Under both proposals, the canon would be redrawn so as explicitly to prohibit disclosure by lawyers of confessions and prior criminal records, or statements of opinion concerning the guilt or innocence of the accused. The ABA revision is the more elaborate, but the differences in detail and phrasing are not of major import, except in one respect to which I shall refer. The ABA Report does, however, propose that the canon may be enforced not only by the usual disciplinary penalties such as disbarment, but by contempt proceedings as well,[63] a proposal with which the ABNY disagrees.[64]

It is in connection with the police, however, that the most important difference between the two reports appears. The ABA field study showed conclusively that, in the pre-arraignment phase of the criminal process, it is the police who are by far the most frequent source of prejudicial publicity.[65] In this there is nothing surprising, and no inference may be drawn that police attitudes are more benighted than those of lawyers or journalists. Prior to arraignment the accused is in police custody, and in the usual case lawyers are not yet involved. If the crime was a shocking one, it is the police who feel community pressure for assurance that the "right" man has been caught, and thus may be led to release news of confessions, prior criminal records, and the other danger-fraught types of publicity that we have noted.

To check the flow of such information from the police, the ABA proposes the adoption of court rules, of a content generally paralleling the amended Canon 20, which would be applicable to police and other law enforcement officials, and enforceable by contempt proceedings. The ABNY, on the other hand, advocates a "code" for the police much the same in substance, but to be voluntarily adopted by the law enforcement agencies rather than promulgated in court rules, and enforceable only by internal administrative measures. As we shall see presently and in more detail, the ABNY Report argues against imposing legal sanctions on the police in the pre-trial period, on grounds of both law and policy.[66]

It is not surprising, accordingly, that the ABNY committee, except for one dissenting member, recommended that no sanctions, legislative or other, be made applicable to the press.[67] Nor is it at all surprising, in the light of constitutional and statutory background we have traced, that the ABA proposals are, in this respect, very narrowly confined to situations in which a criminal trial by jury is actually in process, and a person (who may be a newspaperman) violates a court order not to publish information relating to a hearing from which the public has been excluded, or makes a statement "that goes beyond the public record of the court . . . if the statement is reasonably calculated to affect the outcome of the trial and seriously threatens to have such an effect." [68]

Quite naturally, it is this feature of the ABA Report which has drawn the hottest fires of criticism, and it is the ABA–ABNY divergence on this point which has been most emphasized in the press accounts and comments. Conceptually and constitutionally, of course, the issue is of major significance. But because of the very narrow range of the ABA's contempt proposals as applied to the press, I do not believe the press issue is of nearly as great practical importance as the difference of opinion regarding sanctions applicable to the police.

Regardless of their comparative importance, it is these two matters—sanctions on the police and on the press—which emerge as the core of the controversy within the bar, and I shall now address myself briefly to each.

Sanctions and the Police

The ABNY Report's opposition to court rules directly affecting the police, in pre-trial proceedings, is based in principal part on the belief that the courts have no power to promulgate such rules. Prior to arraignment, says the Report,[69] "the courts lack any power whatsoever over the police"; between arraignment and trial, "as to the police, we find no authority inherent in the courts or the judges to discipline them for alleged breach of their duties as police officers."

The Report is both vague and cursory on the basis for these assertions. There are hints that it is an objection of constitutional dimension, derived from the separation of powers; elsewhere there are murky suggestions that the first amendment is involved.[70] A few irrelevant or inconclusive dicta are cited,[71] but there is no effort to analyze the legitimate scope of the contempt power as applied to the police, and the conclusion must be regarded as lamentably *ex cathedra*.

In reaching the opposite conclusion, the ABA Report is less casual but not wholly satisfactory. Inasmuch as its proposed rule "relating to disclosures by law enforcement officers" is to be applicable "from the time of arrest, issuance of an arrest warrant, or the filing of any complaint, information, or indictment in any criminal matter" within the court's jurisdiction,[72] it is clear that the *charge* is regarded as the thing that brings the contempt power to life.

But the cases relied on in support of this result [73] seem to me to fall short. In the *Shipp* case,[74] wherein the Supreme Court held a state sheriff in contempt, the official was accused of conspiring to lynch a prisoner whose execution had been stayed by Court order pending appeal. In the *Rea* case,[75] the federal court had enjoined a federal agent from giving testimony in a state court about evidence which the agent had seized under an invalid search warrant. Both of these cases involve court action to protect its jurisdiction and prevent abuse or disobedience of its orders. Neither involved pre-trial or pre-arraignment procedures, and thus they can be given little weight as authority for the proposed rule.

The question of the reach of the courts' inherent contempt power is an interesting one, but to my mind it is not of great practical relevance. The courts have hitherto not invoked it for the purposes embodied in the proposed ABA rule, and such an undertaking at this late date will surely get a very cool reception. Police commissioners and the mayors or municipal authorities to whom they are responsible have elective responsibilities and a far broader base of public support than do the courts, even where judges are elected. The summary contempt power has never been a popular judicial institution in this country, and I should think it would be most unwise now to attempt its use on so extensive a footing.

On the other hand, I can see absolutely no constitutional obstacles to a legislative regulation of the matter. Surely, in dealing with police, prosecutors, and other government employees, the legislature confronts no problems either of separation of powers or, in this context, of free speech. The legislature establishes the executive departments, and determines their organization, personnel structure, and ambit of authority; surely it can forbid executive employees to give out information which would threaten the fair and effective functioning of the judicial process.

The ABA Report expresses belief [76] "that a rule of court is preferable to a legislative enactment because the matter falls properly within the judicial sphere and because use of the rule-making power permits greater flexibility whenever the need for change is demonstrated." Whether or not the matter "falls properly within the judicial sphere" is of course the very question at issue; many rules are declared by legislatures and administered by courts, and for reasons already given I believe that such a resolution is best suited in the present instance. So far as concerns "flexibility," there is no reason why a legislative enactment cannot leave ample elbowroom for the exercise of discretion. Indeed, the best of both worlds could be gained here by court rules embodied in legislative enactment, as has been done with the Federal Rules of Criminal and of Civil Procedure. So too, there could be no constitutional objection to contempt proceedings based on statutory authorization, as long as jury trial questions are avoided by limiting non-jury contempt proceedings to the infliction of only minor pains and penalties.

The ABNY Report, however, rejects a legislative approach as "unwise and detrimental to the public interest," observing that: [77] "the prospect, in this pretrial period, of judges of various criminal courts of high and low degree sitting as petty tyrants, handing down sentences of fine and imprisonment for contempt of court against lawyers, policemen, and reporters and editors, is not attractive." Leaving aside for the moment the "reporters and editors," I find this abysmally superficial. The argument either proves nothing or too much, for the prospect of judges doing *anything* as "petty tyrants" is unattractive. If they are conscientiously carrying out a considered legislative mandate, the judges do not act as petty tyrants, and there is no reason why the legislatures may not, in this field, as in others, speak the people's will and call on the courts to give it effect.

Of course, one might take the position that the police should not be discouraged from giving out pre-trial information concerning confessions and the other categories we have noted, but that is not the view of the ABNY Report, which advocates a voluntary police code containing these very restrictions.[78] Assuming that restrictions are desirable, it seems to me that overwhelming arguments favor a considered legislative judgment on their scope and means of enforcement, rather than leaving the whole problem to the discretion of the local police commissioner.

At the policy as distinguished from the legal level, it seems to me that a compelling case has been made for sanction-supported restrictions on the police and other law enforcement officials, to check the flow of prejudicial pre-trial information. Perhaps this may somewhat diminish press opportunities for independent investigation of disputed facts, as in the Whittemore case, but there has been no showing that the contributions of journalists turned Sherlock Holmes are frequent or significant enough to outweigh the prejudicial effects we have observed. To a degree this question interlocks with the next one for consideration: whether or not any restrictions should be made directly applicable to the press.

Sanctions and the Press

As we have seen, the ABNY Report recommends strongly against any sanctions, legislative or judicial, for direct application to the press, and the ABA suggestion is narrowly confined. Limited as they are, however, the ABA proposals raise serious constitutional as well as policy issues.

In support of the constitutionality of its system of limited sanctions on the press, the ABA Report relies heavily on Supreme Court dicta in the *Wood* and *Sheppard* cases which actually do nothing but reserve the question for future determination.[79]

So once again we are thrown back to the same basic questions of constitutional interpretation that we confronted last night. As of when does the Constitution speak? If it means what it was originally meant to mean, the first amendment interposes no absolute barrier to the application of the contempt power—or legislative power, for that matter—to the press.

Such use of the contempt power was well-estabished in England during the eighteenth century, years before the Constitution was adopted.[80] There is not the slightest evidence that the first amendment was intended to limit that practice. The best recent historical analysis of that amendment demonstrated, I thought convincingly, that its framers were chiefly concerned with prior restraints such as licensing, and alleviation of the harsher features of the English law of seditious libel.[81] Compelling evidence that the amendment was *not* designed to affect the reach of the contempt power in protecting the judicial process may be found in decisions, contemporaneous with the Bill of Rights, in both federal and state courts. In 1801 the federal circuit court in Pennsylvania committed William Duane, editor of the *Aurora*.[82] Since this was one of the handful of decisions rendered by the circuit courts created under John Adams' well-known "midnight judges" act,[83] it might be taken *cum grano salis*. But the same stricture can hardly be levelled at a 1788 decision by the Supreme Court of Pennsylvania, in which the contempt commitment was upheld over the explicit argument that it was barred by Section 12 of the Pennsylvania Declaration of Rights, a provision comparable to the soon-to-be first amendment.[84]

After 1831, contempts by publication were barred in the federal courts by the statute of that year spawned by Judge Peck's exuberance. But throughout the nineteenth century and until the *Bridges* decision in 1941,[85] there were quite a number of state court decisions in which the contempt power was exerted, in line with English practice, against the press.[86] In addition, as we have already observed,[87] there were the Baltimore "Tarquinio Rules," adopted just before the *Bridges* decision and ultimately abrogated as a result of it.

But nearly all of these rules and cases applying contempt to publication antedated the application of the first amendment, *via* the fourteenth, to the states, and the Supreme Court's broadening applications of the first amendment in its decisions during the thirties and forties.[88] The *Bridges* case is one of this sequence of cases; it does not purport to bar absolutely use of the contempt power against publications, but disposes of the issue by invocation of Justice Holmes' well-known "clear and present danger" formulation.

In retrospect, it is not a little amusing to see Mr. Justice Black's name attached to the *Bridges* opinion, for in later years it is he who has emerged as the leading court critic of the "clear and present danger" test, as well as of "balancing" and all the other expressions used to qualify the absolute language of the amendment.[89] Even at this early date, however, his attitude was verging on his later absolutism, for he observed (314 U.S. at 263) that "the substantive evil must be extremely serious and the degree of imminence extremely high before utterance can be punished."

Once again we find ourselves in an arena of protracted struggle between Mr. Justice Black and Mr. Justice Frankfurter, and in this instance it is the former who has, at least thus far, emerged victorious. Although the language of the *Bridges* opinion left the door open to a different result given a case wherein the publication posed a clear and present danger to the fairness of a judicial proceeding, neither in that nor any subsequent case [90] has the Court upheld a judgment of contempt by publication.

But no case in the Supreme Court has squarely raised the issue of a contempt judgment's validity in a case involving publicity directly affecting the jury in a criminal case,[91] and the Court's opinions give signs of care to avoid foreclosing such a question. The ABA recommendations are designed to fit within the narrow area thus left open, insofar as the contempt power could be exercised against the press only if a jury trial is in process, and the miscreant publishes something "reasonably calculated to affect the outcome of the trial" which "seriously threatens" such a consequence, or something the publication of which has been prohibited by explicit court order, in order to shield the jury from its knowledge.

Would the ABA Rule survive Supreme Court scrutiny? There is little doubt but that Mr. Justice Black would still turn his thumbs downward: asked by the late Professor Edward Cahn whether the first amendment protects sensational press stories which inflame the public and prevent a fair trial, the Justice replied that he did not think the public inflamed that easily, and that he adhered to the first amendment as an absolute prohibition.[92] But of course Mr. Justice Black's conception of the first amendment has never carried a majority of the Court, and it may fairly be concluded that most members of the Court would find the question a difficult one, and would very likely be closely divided. The Supreme Judicial Court of Massachusetts, confronted recently with a request for an opinion on a bill pending in the Massachusetts legislature which would have authorized contempt by publication, found themselves "unable to predict" what the federal Supreme Court might hold, and begged "to be excused" from answering.[93]

Would legislation providing for criminally enforceable restraints on the press fare better than contempt sanctions imposed under the courts' inherent powers? In both *Bridges* and *Wood* cases, the Court's opinions put some emphasis on the lack of legislative basis for the contempt penalties imposed by the state courts.[94] Strictly speaking, of course a statute cannot eliminate constitutional objections. However, as we have seen, the Court's hostile attitude toward contempt by publication finds small support in the "original understanding," and must be treated rather as an example of "considered consensus." [95] Legislation might serve as a powerful negation of a consensus for total elimination of contempt by publication, and would also provide some political reassurance. If limited to cases of strong threat to jury impartiality, and if provision for jury trial of the contempt itself were required so as to eradicate the unpleasant taste of summary proceedings, the constitutional fate of such legislation would not, I believe, be hopeless.[96]

Dissenting in part from the ABNY Report's conclusions, Mr. Frank S. Hogan, District Attorney of New York, doubted "that the First Amendment precludes a consideration of direct control of the news media, either by legislation or by expanded utilization of the Court's contempt power," and expressed a belief "that carefully and specifically drawn legislation could be enacted which would not offend constitutional limitations." [97] As an abstract proposition I am inclined to agree, but I see little likelihood of legislative action along this line, and so far only a bill introduced in the Massachusetts legislature could be cited to the contrary.[98] The power of the press is stronger in the legislative than the judicial halls, and without compelling reason, which does not yet appear, few legislators will venture to incur the wrath of the Fourth Estate.

Accordingly, I see small chance of either judicial or legislative revival of contempt by publication, with the press as its object. If then, sanctions are to be restricted to the bar, or the bar and police and other law enforcement officers, what will be the practical consequences?

Consequences and Conclusions

On the face of things, they are a bit anomalous. The bar and the police would be under injunction, criminally enforceable, to refrain from divulging information which the press may nevertheless print with immunity if it can be gotten. May this not turn the whole thing into a game of hide and seek? It is the business of a reporter to seek out the news. Perhaps the press will win the game hands down, and in that event the only consequence may be that press reports in the pre-trial period will be attributed to "anonymous but authoritative sources" instead of to the local police chief.

There is, indeed, impressive opinion to this effect, espoused by Mr. Hogan, who believes that there will be cases "where reliance on self-restraint proves futile," [99] and that restrictions applicable only to lawyers and law enforcement officials will not prevent constant leakage of information to the hungry press.[100] I venture to disagree with diffidence; Mr. Hogan's experience, ability, and integrity in the field of law enforcement are universally acknowledged.

But it seems to me that, in this instance, he is overly pessimistic. I draw considerable comfort from the findings in the ABA Report, especially with respect to the situation in New Jersey before and after the announcement of the *Van Duyne* rules: [101]

A 50-day analysis of the Newark *Evening News* prior to the decision showed 22 reports by police of the fact that inculpatory statements had been made. The comparison with the post-*Van Duyne* period, after adjustment for the differing length of the two studies, shows a decrease of 91.4% in the release of such information. The same comparison shows a 95.5% decrease in the release of the content of inculpatory statements. These statistics are derived from a sample of over 1000 local-crime news stories. A good part of the credit for this significant decrease must go to the Newark *Evening News,* which in the wake of *Van Duyne* adopted a general policy against reporting inculpatory statements.

Other information in the ABA Report confirms the beneficial effect of the *Van Duyne* rules [102] which, of course, are directly applicable only to the bar. The statistics in the report also show a significant contrast between San Francisco, where a free system of releasing pre-trial information prevails, and Pittsfield, Massachusetts, where the local *Berkshire Eagle*'s adherence to the Massachusetts bar-press code has resulted in the virtual disappearance of prejudicial publicity.[103]

It is also interesting to learn that in Newark, where the *Evening News* decided to comply with the *Van Duyne* policies, "the information is frequently available to the reporters on an off-the-record basis." [104] This point is closely related to preservation of the positive value of the press as an auxiliary investigating agency. If the press can be relied on *not* to print suspects' confessions—either because such publication is prohibited or by way of voluntary abstention—then information can be given off-the-record which will be useful for such independent inquiries as the newsmen may wish to make. If, however, the newspapers are and feel free to print whatever they find out, off-the-record exchange becomes impossible.

Of course, the promising aspects of this example must not be over-played. Both in Newark and Pittsfield, the improved state of affairs is at least partly if not primarily due to enlightened journalistic practice. It is by no means clear that restrictions on the bar and police would work nearly as well in the setting of a press hostile to such limitations.

There is another facet of the matter which I find even more troublesome. The prosecution and law enforcement officials are government employees, subject to executive and legislative controls which pose no first amendment problems. But defense counsel are not employees, and are answerable for what they say only as members of the bar. The press is not the sole protege of the first amendment; lawyers, too, draw from it certain, though not unlimited, rights of speech, even in their professional capacities.

Some newspapermen are also members of the bar. As long as they are functioning exclusively as reporters or in some other journalistic capacity, I suppose we would all agree that they should not be under any greater restrictions on what they can write and publish than any other newsmen.

But suppose we are concerned with a member of the bar who is not a journalist and neither is he engaged in criminal practice but who, as do some of our well-known television characters, makes a pursuit of free-lance criminal investigation. Should he not be as broadly entitled to divulge information he obtains as is a newsman? Surely membership in the Fourth Estate does not entitle one to a broader protection under the first amendment than is enjoyed by any other citizen.

What reasons may be advanced for greater restrictions on a defense counsel than on members of the bar not involved in the particular case? [105] He, like the prosecution and police, has access, through his client, to facts and circumstances which may not be admissible in evidence, and which may be prejudicial. He can, though with much less leverage, make statements intended to create a community opinion which might taint selection of an impartial jury. No doubt, as an officer of the court, he can be required to refrain from prejudicial divulgences.

But is not the situation quite different if the press with impunity publishes material that is damaging to his client? Must he trust in the efficacy of remedial action by the court, which is powerless to impose any sanction on the offending journals, in view of the acknowledged inadequacy, in many circumstances, of such devices as change of venue? May he not, under such circumstances and if he thinks his client's interests so require, resort to "self-help" by making public information of a countervailing nature, to redress the balance?

I suppose that Canon 20 or any other regulation of professional conduct, like any judicial or legislative rule or enactment or action, is subject to constitutional limitations, including the first amendment. If the *Bridges* case is still law, the "clear and present danger" test is the touchstone of permissibility in this area. All I am suggesting is that the application of that standard might yield very different results when a lawyer, whether on the prosecution or the defense side of the table, is endeavoring to salvage a modicum of impartiality in an atmosphere which the press has already prejudiced, than when the lawyer is himself the agent of the initial distortion. These considerations apply, in point of policy, to prosecution and defense alike. In the case of government employees they can be dealt with as a matter of legislative policy, but with private counsel, it seems to me, constitutional limitations must also be reckoned with.

I call to your attention the initial sentence of Canon 20, as it appears in the amended version proposed in the ABNY Report: [106]

We believe that members of the bar have a duty to refrain from originating the same types of statements *which we believe should not be originated by or appear in the press,* or otherwise be published (italics supplied).

If such matter should not appear in the press, why should the newsmen escape the sanctions to be fastened on the lawyer or policeman who does the divulging? And if the press is free to print these statements, can defense counsel validly or fairly be penalized for taking counteraction?

I confess that I have no answers to these questions that satisfy me in conceptual terms. On the pragmatic level, I am less troubled. Criminally enforceable restrictions on the press are of dubious value, and altogether improbable of enactment in any event. Sanctions applicable to the bar and police are much more feasible, and offer some hope of mitigating the worst abuses.

In the search for wise particularization of such sanctions, it seems to me that the ABA Report has taken a long first step. But the problem does not yield readily to precise calculation; it is, indeed, a draftsman's graveyard. There is great need for flexibility, so that appropriate allowance can be made for variant circumstances—for example, situations such as I have just described, where press accounts have already caused troublesome prejudice, and contradiction or explanation appears to be the least unsatisfactory remedy.

Then, too, there are problems which probably lie

beyond the reach of rules and sanctions. I have here a clipping from the front page of *The New York Times*,[107] carrying a two-column photograph of an Army sergeant in the firm grip of FBI agents, charged with soliciting a bribe in connection with draft deferment of a professional football player. The picture does not appear to have been posed, and none of the guides or codes, so far as I know, would inhibit publishing it. Yet, if the presumption of innocence means anything, it is hard to conceive how it might be more effectively flouted than by such a picture and story, which must do the suspect terrible harm even if he is subsequently acquitted.

All of which leads me to say, in conclusion, that rules and sanctions may contribute to, but cannot constitute the greater part of, a solution of our problem. There is, indeed, no "solution" in any final or semi-final sense.

We may, however, hope for a wider awareness and better understanding of the question, and the Warren Report has been a powerful stimulus to that end. Of its first fruits, the ABA Report is, I believe, the most enlightening and valuable, whether or not one accepts its recommendations.

POSTSCRIPT ON DEVELOPMENTS,
APRIL, 1967, TO APRIL, 1968

During the year that has passed since the presentation at Ohio State University, the two principal developments have been: (1) revision of the ABA Report's recommendations and approval of the amended recommendations by the Association's House of Delegates; and (2) publication of a report on the free press–fair trial issue by a committee of the Judicial Conference of the United States.

The Amended ABA *Recommendations.*—In July, 1967, the ABA Advisory Committee on Fair Trial and Free Press issued a pamphlet entitled "Revisions of Tentative Draft," in which the recommended standards, discussed in the text, were set forth in amended form, together with a commentary on the changes. In December, 1967 the Committee issued a substantially identical pamphlet entitled "Proposed Final Draft."

For the most part, the changes were in the nature of technically perfecting amendments which did not significantly alter the substance of the recommendations. In the portion pertaining to the revision of Canon 20, however, the Committee abandoned its earlier proposal that violations be punishable by contempt as well as by the usual bar disciplinary sanctions. In the commentary (Proposed Final Draft, at 21) this change was explained on the basis that "jurisdictions differ on the availability of contempt in such a case" and that "the possibility of professional discipline—reprimand, suspension, or disbarment—seemed adequate to insure compliance." The change seems to me desirable, in that it will eliminate controversy by abandoning a point of no great practical significance.

By far the most important departure from the original recommendations was made in the section dealing with police and other law enforcement officials. Whereas the original proposal called for the adoption of rules of court enforceable against the police by contempt, the amended plan (Proposed Final Draft, at 22–23) envisages that "the entire matter be dealt with at the outset by department regulation and that with respect to the period from arrest to the completion of trial, a rule of court *or* legislative enactment be resorted to only if a law enforcement agency fails to adopt and adhere to the substance of the recommended regulation 'within a reasonable time.'" Furthermore, while the original report (at 102) expressed a definite preference for regulation of the police by rule of court rather than by legislative enactment, the commentary to the amended draft (at 22 n.23) is neutral on this point.

The commentary justifies the change on the grounds that a number of law enforcement agencies have shown "a willingness to take steps toward self-regulation" and that "some doubt has been expressed about the propriety of a rule of court that purports to govern, even in a limited way, the conduct of the executive branch." My own confidence in adequate self-regulation by the police does not match that espoused by the Committee, but I welcome the more hospitable attitude toward legislative treatment which the amended recommendations manifest.

The amended recommendations came before the Association at its meeting in Chicago in February, 1968. Before voting, the House of Delegates heard criticism of the proposals from news and television executives, who particularly complained that the Association was proposing to act without awaiting the results of the ANPA study of the effects of publicity on juries. On February

20, 1968 the House of Delegates approved the recommendations by a voice vote, after turning down a proposal for a year's delay by a vote of 176 to 68. Editorial reaction was generally negative; *The New York Times,* in an above-the-battle comment, advised the news media to "play it cool."

Report on the "Free Press–Fair Trial" issue by the Committee on the Operation of the Jury System of the Judicial Conference of the United States.—This report was approved by the Committee, chaired by Circuit Judge Irving R. Kaufman, on January 26, 1968. It is the product of deliberation by a subcommittee of seven federal circuit and district judges, commencing in September, 1966, in the course of which spokesmen for the news media were heard.

The Report proposes that the controls it envisages be implemented by local federal district court rules. These would cover three areas: (1) release of prejudicial information by members of the bar of the court in question; (2) comparable releases by courthouse personnel; (3) special rules governing the trial proceedings in sensational cases where prejudical press influences are to be feared.

The second of these is of minor significance. The first proposition is substantially the same as that approved in the *Van Duyne* case. The rule proposed to be applied to the bar is, however, drawn *verbatim* from the comparable rule in the ABA Proposed Final Draft. The third proposal is cast in very general terms, and merely recognizes the possible desirability in "a widely publicized or sensational case," of special orders on such matters as extra-judicial statements by participants in the trial, the arrangements in the courtroom, and the handling of jurors and witnesses.

The Report follows the ABNY lead in eschewing any recommendations for direct restraint on the press or law enforcement agencies. Of course, since its purview was limited to federal law enforcement, the permissible range of application of the contempt power is greatly narrowed by the 1831 statute. Press reaction to the Report was generally favorable, and that is hardly surprising.

Notes

NOTES

Introduction

1. Miranda v. Arizona, 384 U.S. 436 (1966).

2. Vignera v. New York [No. 760], 384 U.S. 436, 493–94 (1966).

3. The colloquy is set forth in 34 LW 3299 (Mar. 8, 1966), and in MEDALIE, FROM ESCOBEDO TO MIRANDA—THE ANATOMY OF A SUPREME COURT DECISION, 123 (1966).

4. A MODEL CODE OF PRE-ARRAIGNMENT PROCEDURE (Tent. Draft No. 1, March 1, 1966, of the American Law Institute).

5. HAND, THE BILL OF RIGHTS, 1–30 (1958).

6. M. R. COHEN, THE FAITH OF A LIBERAL, 178–80, 182–85, and 192 (1946); CARR, DEMOCRACY AND THE SUPREME COURT, 124 (1936); BOUDIN, GOVERNMENT BY JUDICIARY (1932); cf. Eakin v. Raub, 12 S. & R. 330 (Pa. 1825).

7. WECHSLER, PRINCIPLES, POLITICS, AND FUNDAMENTAL LAW, 15–28 (1961).

8. Cf. JACKSON, THE SUPREME COURT IN THE AMERICAN SYSTEM OF GOVERNMENT, 80–83 (1955); BICKEL, THE LEAST DANGEROUS BRANCH, 111–98 (1962); Gunther, The Subtle Vices of the 'Passive Virtues'—A Commentary on Principle and Expediency in Judicial Review, 64 COL. L. REV. 1 (1964).

9. Adamson v. California, 332 U.S. 46, 71–75 and 92–123 (1947). Mr. Justice Black's historical conclusion did not escape cogent and, to me, compelling negative analysis. See Fairman, Does the Fourteenth Amendment Incorporate the Bill of Rights? The Original Understanding, 2 STAN. L. REV. 5 (1949).

10. U.S. Const. art. I, § 10, par. 3. Mr. Justice Black surely would have no quarrel; in his most recent pronouncement on this question, dissenting in Berger v. New York, 388 U.S. 41 (1967), he writes (at 87) : "Of course, where the Constitution has stated a broad purpose to be accomplished under any circumstances, we must consider that modern science has made it necessary to use new means in accomplishing the framers' goal. A good illustration of this is the Commerce Clause which gives Congress power to regulate commerce between the states however it may be carried on, whether by ox wagons or jet planes."

11. See his dissenting opinion in Jackson v. Denno, 378 U.S. 368, 403 (1964).

12. Ferguson v. Georgia, 365 U.S. 570, 582 (1961).

13. The Georgia statutes, while disqualifying the defendant as a witness, allowed him to make an unsworn statement, immune from cross-examination. In the *Ferguson* case, the defendant did not seek to testify under oath, but asked to give his unsworn statement in answer to direct questions by his counsel. The trial court sustained the prosecution's objections to the participation of counsel. Reversing the judgment of conviction, the Supreme Court held (365 U.S. at 569) only that the denial of counsel in giving the unsworn statement violated the fourteenth amendment. Justices Frankfurter and Clark concurred in the result, but on the ground that the statutory disqualification of the defendant as a witness was unconstitutional.

14. Griswold v. Connecticut, 381 U.S. 479, 516 (1965). In the *Berger* case, 388 U.S. 41 at p. 87, he put his point even more categorically: "I believe it is the Court's duty to interpret these [Constitutional] grants and limitations so as to carry out as nearly as possible the original intent of the framers. But I do not believe that it is our duty to go further than the framers did on the theory that the judges are charged with responsibility for keeping the Constitution 'up to date.'"

15. Gideon v. Wainwright, 372 U.S. 335 (1963).

16. See Brief for the Petitioner in Gideon v. Wainwright, No. 155, Oct. Term 1962, p. 29; *cf.* Kamisar, *Equal Justice in the Gatehouses and Mansions of American Criminal Procedure,* in CRIMINAL JUSTICE IN OUR TIME, p. 92 n. 262 (University of Virginia Press,

1965) ; Kamisar, Book Review of *Gideon's Trumpet* by Anthony Lewis, 78 HARV. L. REV. 478, 479 (1964) .

17. 380 U.S. 609 (1965) .

18. See Tehan v. Shott, 382 U.S. 406, 417–18 (1966) .

19. Mapp v. Ohio, 367 U.S. 643 (1963) .

20. State v. Sheridan, 121 Ia. 164, 96 N.W. 730 (1903) .

21. Eighteen states had adopted the exclusionary rule by 1949. See Wolf v. Colorado, 338 U.S. 25, 33–39 (1949) . By 1960, several more states had adopted it, and the Court observed that "the movement toward exclusion has been halting but seemingly inexorable." Elkins v. United States, 364 U.S. 206, 219 (1960) . In holding the rule constitutionally binding on the states in 1961, the Court referred directly to the experience of the states, particularly California. Mapp v. Ohio, 367 U.S. 643 at 650–53; People v. Cahan, 44 Cal.2d 434, 282 P.2d 905 (1955) .

22. Escobedo v. Illinois, 378 U.S. 478 (1964).

23. People v. Donovan, 13 N.Y.2d 148 (1963) ; *cf.* People v. DiBiasi, 7 N.Y.2d 544 (1960) .

24. Friendly, *The Bill of Rights as a Code of Criminal Procedure,* 53 CAL L. REV. 929, 943–44, 946 (1965) ; BEANEY, THE RIGHT TO COUNSEL IN AMERICAN COURTS, 21 (1955) ; *cf.* Bram v. United States, 168 U.S. 532 (1897) .

25. Miranda v. Arizona, 384 U.S. 436, 467–79 (1966) . Following the *Escobedo* decision, however, three states conditioned the admissibility of pre-arraignment statements on a showing that the accused had been advised of his right to remain silent and to consult counsel. People v. Dorado, 398 P.2d 361 (Cal. 1965) ; People v. Neely, 398 P.2d 482 (Ore. 1965) ; State v. Dujour, 206 A.2d 82 (R.I. 1965) .

26. United States v. Lovett, 328 U.S. 303 (1946) .

27. 328 U.S. 303 at 321.

28. *E.g.,* Act for the Attainder of Thomas Fitzgerald, 26 Hen. VIII, c.6; note 72 YALE L.J. 330 (1962) .

29. Cummings v. Missouri, 4 Wall. 277 (1866) ; *Ex parte* Garland, 4 Wall. 333 (1866) .

30. United States v. Archie Brown, 381 U.S. 437 (1965).

31. See Mr. Justice Field's opinion in Cummings v. Missouri, 4 Wall. at 319–20, wherein he uses "reasonable relation" as the test of the validity of the statute there held unconstitutional as an attainder. The soundness of Mr. Justice Frankfurter's distinction, as applied to attainder, has been subjected to sharp historical-analytic criticism. Note 72 YALE L.J. 330, 341–43 (1962).

32. Murray v. Hoboken L. & I. Co., 18 How. 272, 277 (1855).

33. In the same colloquy with Mr. Siegel that produced his question about the A.L.I. CODE (*supra* note 3), Mr. Justice Black declared: "We long ago got over the idea that this country has got to adopt every old principle of the common law."

34. *E.g.,* as set forth in his dissent in Griswold v. Connecticut, 381 U.S. 479, 508–27 (1965).

35. Medalie, *supra* note 3, at 88, 94, 104, 116–17, 121, and 147.

36. McCulloch v. Maryland, 4 Wheat. 316, 406 (1819).

37. In the *McCulloch* case, however, Marshall leaned heavily (4 Wheat. at 401–402) on the action of the First Congress, in which sat many of the framers, as manifesting the framers' understanding that the constitutionally-granted powers of Congress were broad enough to include the incorporation of a national bank.

38. Slaughter-House Cases, 16 Wall. 36 (1873) ; Civil Rights Cases, 109 U.S. 3 (1883).

39. *Ex parte* Bain, 121 U.S. 1, 12 (1887).

40. 1 W.&M. 2 (1688).

41. Trials for High Treason of Lieut. Col. Edward Marcus Despard et al. (Birmingham, 1803) at p. 46: "It only remains for me to pronounce the dreadful sentence which the law denounces against your crime, which is, 'That you, and each of you, (here his Lordship named the prisoners severally,) be taken to the place from whence you came, and from thence you are to be drawn on hurdles to the place of execution, where you are to be hanged by the neck, but not until you are dead; for while you are still living, your bodies are to be taken down, your bowels torn out, and burnt before your faces; your heads are to be then cut off, and your bodies divided each into four quarters, and your heads and quarters to be

then at the King's disposal; and may the Almighty God have mercy on your souls.' "

42. Robinson v. California, 370 U.S. 660 (1962).

43. Trop v. Dulles, 356 U.S. 86, 100–01 (1958), citing Weems v. United States, 217 U.S. 349, 373 (1910) to the same effect.

44. Harper v. Virginia Bd. of Elections, 383 U.S. 663, 669 (1966).

45. Mr. Justice McKenna in Weems v. United States, 217 U.S. at 373.

Part I

1. *Supra* at p. 13.

2. *Supra* at p. 7.

3. See, *e.g., Wiretapping* Hearings before Subcommittee No. 5 of the House Committee on the Judiciary on H.R. 762, 867, 4513, 4728, and 5096 (84th Cong., 1st Sess.) *passim.*

4. Mapp v. Ohio, 367 U.S. 643 (1961).

5. *Cf.* Gouled v. United States, 255 U.S. 298 (1921) and Warden v. Hayden, 387 U.S. 294 (1967). The latter case is discussed *infra* at 93–95.

6. 367 U.S. 643 at 661–62.

7. *Consent Searches: A Reapprasial after Miranda v. Arizona,* 67 Col. L. Rev. 130 (1967).

8. For a very recent example, see Camara v. Municipal Court, 387 U.S. 523 (discussed *infra* at p. 95), wherein, *per* Mr. Justice White, the Court said (at 528–29): ". . . one governing principle, justified by history and by current experience, has been consistently followed: except in certain carefully defined classes of cases, a search of private property . . . is 'unreasonable' unless it has been authorized by a valid search warrant." See also McDonald v. United States, 335 U.S. 451, 453 (1948) ; Johnson v. United States, 333 U.S. 10, 14 (1948).

9. *E.g.,* Mr. Justice Douglas, dissenting in McCray v. Illinois, 386 U.S. 300, 316 (1967).

10. Harris v. United States, 331 U.S. 145, 162 (1947). In Davis v. United States, 328 U.S. 582 (1946), again in dissent, he went even further (at 605), invoking the warrant clause of the fourth amendment as "the key to what the framers had in mind by prohibiting 'unreasonable' searches and seizures," which was "that all seizures without judicial authority were deemed 'unreasonable.'"

11. Harris v. United States, *supra* at 195–98.

12. Trial Manual for the Defense of Criminal Cases, Preliminary Draft No. 1 (Sept. 29, 1966), Joint Committee on Continuing Legal Education of the American Law Institute and the American Bar Association, 28.

13. Entick v. Carrington, 19 How. St. Tr. 1029, 1067 (C.P. 1765). On this, the late Judge Hough commented: "This I take to mean that the search had crept into the warrant, as 'warrant' is the ancient common-law name for the authority to arrest, and, by the time Lord Camden gave his historic judgment, justices of the peace had at common law authority to issue search warrants. . . ." United States v. Maresca, 266 Fed. 713, 721 (S.D.N.Y. 1920).

14. INSTITUTES, Book 4, cap. 31, at 176–77 (1641).

15. POTTER, HISTORICAL INTRODUCTION TO ENGLISH LAW 207–10 (1932).

16. HALE, PLEAS OF THE CROWN, 149–50. Published posthumously like all other legal works of Hale (1609–76), this passage refers (critically) to Coke's FOURTH INSTITUTE, and thus postdates 1641.

17. The process is now obsolete, but was used in the United States well into the 19th century. For early American examples see Frisbie v. Butler, Kirby 213 (Conn. 1787); Grumon v. Raymond, 1 Conn. 40, 6 Am. Dec. 200 (1814); Bell v. Clapp, 10 Johns. 263, 6 Am. Dec. 339 (N.Y. 1813).

18. The statute is 9 Edw. III, St. II, ch. 11. My account of the history of statutory warrants is based largely on LASSON, THE HISTORY AND DEVELOPMENT OF THE FOURTH AMENDMENT TO THE UNITED STATES CONSTITUTION, 23 *et seq.* (1937).

19. 13 and 14 Char. II, ch. 33, sec. 15.

20. For an early but inconclusive challenge see Rex v. Earbury, 2 Barn. K.B. 346, 94 Eng. Rep. 544 (1733), wherein the court approved the authority to arrest under the Secretary's warrant, but declined to pass upon the legality of the seizure of documents.

21. The order is quoted in Lasson, *supra* note 18, at 29 n.58.

22. 12 Car. 2 c. 19 (1660) and 13 and 14 Car. 2 c.11 § 5 (1662).

23. From a letter to William Tudor written many years later (29 May, 1817). The passage is often quoted, including the famous phrase: "Then and there the child independence was born." See, *e.g.*, 2 LEGAL PAPERS OF JOHN ADAMS 107 (Wroth & Zobel ed. 1965).

24. *Loc. cit. supra* n.16.

25. The revenue "writs of assistance" as authorized in 1660 were issuable by the Lord Treasurer, any of the Barons of the Exchequer, or the Chief Magistrate of the Port where the search was to be made. By that time the court of Exchequer had acquired a judicial status, but its origin was semi-administrative and fiscal. Potter, *op. cit. supra* n.15. Other legislation authorized the Commissioners of Excise to issue search warrants for uncustomed goods. Cooper v. Boot, 4 Dougl. 339, 99 Eng. Rep. 911 (K.B. 1785).

26. POLLOCK AND MAITLAND, THE HISTORY OF ENGLISH LAW 582–83 (2d ed. 1903).

27. WILLIAM SHEPPARD, THE OFFICES OF CONSTABLES, ch. 8, § 2, no. 4 (London, c. 1650). See also SAUNDERS WELCH, OBSERVATIONS ON THE OFFICE OF CONSTABLE, 12, 14 (1754).

28. Dillon v. O'Brien, 16 Cox C.C. 245 (Exch. Ireland, 1887), and Elias v. Pasmore (1934) 2 K.B. 164, 50 T.L.R. 196, discussed *infra* at pp. 60–61.

29. George Montagu Dunk, Earl Halifax and lord of the King's privy council and secretary of state.

30. For an example of the earlier use of such a warrant, in addition to Rex v. Earbury, *supra* note 20, see The Trial of Colonel Algernon Sidney, IX Howell St. Tr. 813 (K.B. 1683).

31. Pratt had already released Wilkes (who had been arrested and committed to the Tower) on habeas corpus, on the ground of Wilkes' privilege as a member of Parliament. Thereafter, by a joint vote of both Houses, Parliament resolved that its privilege did not

extend to seditious libel. The Case of John Wilkes, XIX Howell St. Tr. 981 (C.P. 1763).

32. Huckle v. Money, 2 Wils. K.B. 205, 95 Eng. Rep. 768 (1763). The verdict in this case was for £300; the plaintiff was a journeyman printer working for Dryden Leach, the principal printer plaintiff.

33. Wilkes v. Wood, Lofft 1, 98 Eng. Rep. 489 (C.P., Westminster, 6 December 1763). Wilkes later collected £4000 damages from Halifax. Wilkes v. Halifax, XIX Howell St. Tr. 1401 (1769).

34. William Murray Mansfield (1705–93), a Scotsman, married an earl's daughter, rose at the bar, and after serving as solicitor-general and attorney-general (in which capacity he led the House of Commons) was made a baron and appointed Chief Justice of the Court of King's Bench in 1756. Elevated to an earldom twenty years later, he several times declined the lord chancellorship.

35. Charles Pratt (1714–94), whose father had been Chief Justice of the Court of Kings Bench under George I, made his early reputation at the bar by defending a bookseller charged with libel. He was appointed Attorney General in 1757, and was knighted and appointed Chief Justice of the Court of Common Pleas in 1762, so that he was new to the bench when the *Wilkes* and *Entick* cases came before him. He was made a baron (as Lord Camden) in 1765, and became Lord Chancellor the following year. His vigorous opposition to the government's policies *vis-à-vis* the North American colonies led to his resignation in 1770. As an ardent and outspoken procolonialist, his name was taken by the cities of Camden, S. Car. and Camden, New Jersey.

36. Money, Watson, & Blackmore v. Dryden Leach, 3 Burr. 1742, 97 Eng. Rep. 1075 (K.B.1765), also reported *sub nom.* Leach v. Money, Watson & Blackmore, XIX How. St. Trs. 1002 at 1028 (1765). Compare Mansfield's later decision in Cooper v. Boot, *supra* note 25, a case involving a regularly issued warrant for uncustomed tea. No tea was found, and the victim of the search sued the revenue officers in trespass. Holding for the defendants, Mansfield rejected the theory of absolute liability; it would be a "solecism," he thought, if "the regular execution of a legal warrant shall be in trespass." Liability there might be if the officers acted with malice, and the case might also be different were it a warrant for stolen goods, but this warrant was "for the benefit of the public, and it is for their benefit that the parties may proceed safely on reasonable grounds."

37. XIX How. St. Trs. 1026–27.

38. XIX How. St. Trs. 1029 (C.P. 1765).

39. XIX How. St. Trs. 1062–63.

40. *Id.* at 1063.

41. Money v. Leach, *supra* note 36, was decided a few weeks before *Entick* v. *Carrington.* Lord Camden cited it, *sub nomine* "Case of the General Warrants" for two points: (1) the "messenger" must obey the terms of the warrant, and can get no comfort from it if he departs from its requirements, and (2) the Secretary of State's past practice of issuing "general" warrants did not establish their validity, since no objection to them had been pressed to the point of judicial decision.

42. XIX How. St. Trs. 1063–72.

43. *Id.* at 1073.

44. *Id.* at 1065.

45. XVI The Parliamentary History of England 207–10 (1813).

46. *Supra* at pp. 26–27 and note 22.

47. 1 Anne St. 1, c. 8, sec. 5, cited in Horace Gray's appendix in Quincy (*infra* note 49) at 397 n.5.

48. 7 and 8 Wm. III, ch. 22, sec. 6, cited in Lasson, *supra* note 18, at 53 n.13.

49. The two principal sources for the papers and reports of argument are Quincy's Reports 51–57 and Appendix I, 395–540 (Mass. 1761–72); and 2 Legal Papers of John Adams 106–47 (Wroth and Zobel ed. 1965). The appendix in the Quincy reports, written by Horace Gray, is invaluable, as are the notes to the Adams papers. There is a good account of the litigation in Lasson, 51–66 *supra* note 18. Quincy reported only the second argument, in November 1761, *sub nom.* "Paxton's Case," after Nicholas Paxton, the Surveyor for the Port of Boston. Adams reported the earlier and more important argument, which began February 24, 1761, and lasted several days.

50. *E.g.,* Thacher's argument that the Superior Court had "disclaimed the authority of the Exchequer." See Quincy at 54; Legal Papers of John Adams at 125.

51. Legal Papers of John Adams at 141–44.

52. *Id.* at 127 and 144; Quincy at 56. The famous decision of Coke cited by Otis is *Dr. Bonham's Case,* 8 Co. Rep. 1136, 118, 77 Eng. Rep. 646, 652–53 (C.P. 1610).

53. Legal Papers of John Adams at 115; Quincy at 57.

54. Quincy, appendix at 500–511; Lasson, *supra* note 18 at 73–77.

55. Compare the handling of the legal-political problems raised by the first Congressional investigatory resolution (to inquire into General St. Clair's defeat by the Indians in 1791), when Washington and his cabinet looked for precedent to Pitt's speeches and the Commons' investigation of the Walpole regime. TAYLOR, GRAND INQUEST at 8–10 and 22–24 (1955).

56. I have seen no evidence that the Otis and Thacher arguments in the 1761 writs of assistance case were known to the lawyers and judges involved during the next four years in the *Wilkes* and *Entick* cases.

57. See Camden (then Pratt) in Huckle v. Money, 2 Wils. K.B. 207, and in Wilkes v. Wood, 98 Eng. Rep. 498; Mansfield in Money v. Leach, XIX How. St. Trs. 1026–27.

58. See Wilkes v. Wood, 98 Eng. Rep. 498; Entick v. Carrington, XIX How. St. Trs. 1067.

59. Entick v. Carrington, *loc cit. supra.*

60. Freeman v. Bluet, 12 Wils. 3, 12 Mod. 395, 88 Eng. Rep. 1403 (K.B. 1700). The thrust of the case is as cited by Otis, but it involved a "precept" for replevin, not a stolen goods warrant.

61. Legal Papers of John Adams, *supra* at 125, 128, and 139.

62. Lasson, *supra* note 18, at 79–82.

63. Article XIV of the Declaration of Rights of 1780.

64. As the account in Lasson, *loc. cit. supra* note 62, shows, the House never actually agreed to the revised wording, but the Senate and the ratifying states did so.

65. *Supra* at p. 23.

66. Despite the colonists' righteous indignation against the general warrants, and the embodiment of libertarian views in the

early constitutions, their principles sometimes collapsed under the stress of the Revolutionary War. In 1777 the Continental Congress authorized the seizure of persons, including many Quakers, whose political inclinations were suspect, "together with all such papers in their possession as may be of a political nature." The ensuing abuses are described in Lasson, *op. cit. supra* note 18, at 76–78. Compare, however, the Massachusetts statutes for the disarming of Tories, the apprehension of deserters from the Continental Army, and the seizure of British goods, which were drawn in general accordance with the requirements as stated in the 1780 Constitution. Mass Acts 1776, ch. VIII, p. 31; 2 Nov. 1781, ch. XIII, p. 103; 8 Nov. 1782, ch. XV, p. 191. Contemporaneous statutes of like purpose in New York and Pennsylvania were comparably limited. N.Y. Stat. 13 April 1782, ch. XXXIX; Penn. Sess. Laws 2 Jan. 1778, p. 94.

67. *E.g.,* the statutes involved in Halsted v. Brice, 13 Mo. 120 (1850) and Humes v. Taber, 1 R.1.464 (1850). Most search warrant statutes today are broadly enough drawn to encompass the old stolen goods type, but the emphasis is on criminal law enforcement rather than private restitution. In England the common-law warrant was given criminal statutory form in 1782. 22 Geo. III c. 58.

68. *E.g.,* Mass. Acts 1751, ch. VI, p. 421; Mass. Act of Nov. 17, 1786, ch. XIX, p. 526, and June 19, 1801, and June 20, 1809, ch. XXXV, p. 44; N.Y. Laws 13 Apr. 1782, ch. XXXIX, and 15 Mar. 1788, ch. LXXXI; Pa. Sess. Laws 5 Apr. 1785, p. 563, and 28 Mar. 1787, p. 257, and 16 Mar. 1809, ch. XXXIV.

69. *E.g.,* 1 Stat. 43, July 31, 1789; 1 Stat. 207, Mar. 3, 1791; 3 Stat. 199, Feb. 4, 1815; 12 Stat. 740, Mar. 3, 1863; 14 Stat. 546, Mar. 2, 1867. The federal statutes authorizing search warrants are listed and categorized in an appendix to Mr. Justice Frankfurter's dissenting opinion in Davis v. United States, 328 U.S. 582, 616 (1946).

70. 12 Stat. 579, July 16, 1862 (lottery tickets and gaming in the District of Columbia, authorizing police search, on authority of the Superintendent, without a warrant) ; 17 Stat. 599, Mar. 3, 1873 (obscene literature) ; 19 Stat. 142, Aug. 14, 1876 (counterfeiting of registered trade marks) ; 26 Stat. 743, Feb. 10, 1893 (counterfeiting of money) .

71. *E.g.,* Sandford v. Nichols, 13 Mass. 286 (1816); Gardner v. Neil, 4 N.Car. 104 (1814); Beaty v. Perkins, 6 Wend. 382 (N.Y. Sup. Ct. 1831); Reed v. Rice, 2 J.J. Marsh, 45 (Ky. 1829); Halsted v. Brice, 13 Mo. 12 (1850); Larthet v. Forgay, 2 La. Ann. 524 (1827); Chipman v. Bates, 15 Vt. 51 (1843); Humes v. Taber, 1 R.I. 464 (1850).

72. People v. Holcomb, 3 Park C.C. 656 (N.Y. Sup. Ct. 1858).

73. *E.g.,* Robinson v. Richardson, 13 Gray 454 (Mass. 1859).

74. With the notable exception, needless to say, of Boyd v. United States, 116 U.S. 616 (1886), discussed *infra* at pp. 53–55.

75. Robinson v. Richardson, *supra* note 73; *cf.* People v. Chiagles, 237 N.Y. 193, 195 (1927), per Cardozo, J.: "unreasonable in the light of common law traditions."

76. In Wakely v. Hart, 6 Binney 316 (Pa. 1814), the plaintiff sued the constable in trespass for arresting him without a warrant, arguing that such arrests were prohibited by the Pennsylvania Constitution. Rejecting the argument, Chief Justice Tilghman observed (at 318): "But it is nowhere said, that there shall be no arrest without warrant. To have said so would have endangered the safety of society." Presumably he would have said the same about the customary search concomitants of a valid arrest.

77. I have found only three American cases prior to 1920 in which warrantless searches incident to arrest are involved, and in all three the validity of a search of the arrestee's person, and seizure of fruits or evidences of his crime, is treated as customary and legitimate practice. Thatcher v. Weeks, 79 Me. 547 (1887); Holker v. Hennessey, 141 Mo. 527 (1897); Houghton v. Bushmann, 47 Barb. 388 (N.Y. Sup. Ct. 1866). In the Missouri case the court said (at 540): "We find no statute of this state giving the arresting officer authority to search a prisoner, but no statute is necessary. The power exists from the nature and objects of the public duty the officer is required to perform."

78. State v. Sheridan, 121 Ia. 164, 96 N.W. 730 (1903).

79. Weeks v. United States, 232 U.S. 383 (1914).

80. See the tabulation in Wolf v. Colorado, 338 U.S. 25, 29, 34–39 (1949), indicating that at that time 16 states had adopted and 31 had rejected the exclusionary rule. Ten years later, half of the

states had adopted the exclusionary rule. Elkins v. United States, 366 U.S. 206, 224–25 (1960).

81. *Supra* at pp. 27–29 and n.77.

82. People v. Chiagles, 237 N.Y. 193 (1927).

83. Oh, for the simpler days of yore! The first case invoked by Judge Cardozo, Thatcher v. Weeks, *supra* n.77, at p. 45, involved an action to recover the value of two drums, seized from the plaintiff when he was arrested for beating them in violation of a city ordinance. After trial the Mayor refused to return the drums, because the plaintiff declared he would beat them again as soon as he got them back. The Supreme Court of Maine ruled that this would not do; the drums were legitimately seized for use as evidence against the plaintiff at his trial, but thereafter must be returned, since drums were not contraband.

84. The first Supreme Court case involving a contested search incident to arrest is Silverthorne Lumber Co. v. United States, 251 U.S. 385 (1920). Note, however, the earlier British case of Dillon v. O'Brien, 16 Cox C.C. (1887).

85. I am indebted for the information above to the Office of the Honorable Frank S. Hogan, District Attorney of New York County.

86. McCray v. Illinois, 386 U.S. 300 (1967).

87. I do not, by this comment, mean to brush aside the possibility of providing practical avenues to compensation for persons victimized by unlawful searches; it may be that a hybrid administrative-judicial proceeding of some sort would best fill this need, which may likewise exist with respect to false arrests.

88. This observation does not apply to other kinds of unwarranted searches recognized by law, such as those of moving vehicles, or (assuming they prove constitutionally viable) those incident to "stop-and-frisk."

89. Or if allowable because of other circumstances, as indicated in note 88 *supra*.

90. See United States v. Poller, 43 F.2d 911 (C.C.A. 2d 1930), wherein Judge Hand (at 913) described it as "unreasonable to suppose that an arrest should give wider latitude of search than a search warrant itself." See also United States v. Lefkowitz, 285 U.S. 452,

464 (1932), and Mr. Justice Frankfurter's dissenting opinion in Davis v. United States, 328 U.S. 582, at 595 (1946).

91. If the execution of the search warrant affords adequate grounds to make an arrest, of course the arrest may furnish the basis for further search. *Cf.* United States v. Kirschenblatt, 14 F.2d 202 (C.C.A.2d, 1926).

92. *Cf.* Rochin v. California, 342 U.S. 165 (1952); Breithaupt v. Abram, 352 U.S. 432 (1957); Schmerber v. California, 384 U.S. 757 (1966).

93. *E.g.*, Harris v. United States, 331 U.S. 145 (1947); Marron v. United States, 275 U.S. 192 (1927); United States v. Rabinowitz, 339 U.S. 57 (1950); Abel v. United States, 362 U.S. 217 (1960); Ker v. California, 374 U.S. 23 (1963). In the only two important British decisions since the *Entick* case, a very broad authority to search the premises of an arrestee was recognized. Dillon v. O'Brien, 16 Cox C.C. 245 (Exch. Ireland 1887), and Elias v. Pasmore, [1934] 2 K.B. 164, 50 T.L.R. 196.

94. Gouled v. United States, 255 U.S. 298, 309 (1921).

95. *E.g.*, Morrison v. United States, 262 F.2d 449 (D.C. Cir. 1958); Hayden v. Warden, 363 F.2d 647 (C.A. 4, 1966). The latter case was reviewed by the United States Supreme Court in a decision repudiating the *Gouled* rule; the Court's decision is discussed *infra* at pp. 93–95.

96. See the discussion of the lower federal court and state court cases in the note entitled *Evidentiary Searches: The Rule and the Reason*, 54 Geo. L.J. 593, 606–621 (1966).

97. Note—*Limitations on Seizure of Evidentiary Objects: A Rule in Search of a Reason*, 20 U. of Chi. L. Rev., 319 (1953); Kamisar, *Wiretapping and Eavesdropping: A Professor's View*, 44 Minn. L. Rev. 891, 914–18 (1960).

98. State v. Bisaccia, 45 N.J. 504, 213 A.2d 185 (1965) (Weintraub, C. J.); People v. Thayer, 63 Cal.2d 635, 408 P.2d 108 (1965) (Traynor, J.); Hayden v. Warden, 363 F.2d 647 (C.A.4, 1966) (Haynsworth).

99. *I.e.*, prior to the *Mapp* case, the evidence need not have been excluded even if unlawfully seized. The statutes were an effort to

legitimatize the seizure of "mere evidence" despite the ruling in the *Gouled* case, n.94 *supra*. Col. Rev. Stats. 1963, c. 23, Rules Crim. Proc. 41 (b)(3); Ga. Code Ann. Secs. 27–301 (d) and (e) ; Ill. Rev. Stats., c.38, secs. 108–1 (d) and 108–1 (d) and 108–3 (a) ; West's La. Stats. Ann. Title IV arts. 161 (3) and 165; Mich. Pub. Acts 1966 No. 189, Mich. Stats. Ann. sec. 28, 1259 (2)(d) ; Minn. Stats. Ann. sec. 626.07 (5) ; Neb. Rev. Stats. sec. 29–813; Nev. Rev. Stats. secs. 179.010 and 179.020 (4) ; N.Car. Gen. Stats. sec. 15–25.2; Ore. Rev. Stats. sec. 141.010 (2) . Five other states and the Territory of Hawaii had comparable statutes before the *Mapp* case. West's Ann. Cal. Code, tit.12, secs. 1542 and 1524 (4) ; Hawaii Rev. Laws; tit.30, sec. 255–17; Baldwin's Ohio Dev. Code secs. 2905.23 and 2905.24; Vt. Stats. Ann. sec. 4701 (9) ; Wash. Rev. Code sec. 10.79.015 (3) ; Wis. Stats. Ann., tit. 46, sec. 963.02 (10) .

100. See the tabulation and citations in Mr. Justice Clark's opinion in Berger v. New York, 388 U.S. 41, 47–49 (1967). The six states are California, Maryland, Massachusetts, Nevada, New York, and Oregon.

101. *Eg.*, N.Y. Code Crim. Prac. §813–a.

102. XIX How. St. Trs. at 1073.

103. Boyd v. United States, 116 U.S. 616 (1886) .

104. 18 Stat. 187, Act of June 22, 1874 §5.

106. At least in retrospect, the reliance on the fourth amendment so clearly seems misplaced that one must wonder that Justice Bradley's opinion commanded the concurrence not only of Justices Field and Harlan, but also of Justice Horace Gray, who had written the learned appendix on writs of assistance in the Quincy reports, n.49 *supra*. Mr. Justice Bradley's rationale (116 U.S. at 622) is based on a confusion of consequence and means.

107. Acts of March 2, 1867 and March 3, 1863, respectively 14 Stat. 547 and 12 Stat. 737.

108. 116 U.S. at 635–38. The principal lower court decision thus disapproved is Stockwell v. United States, Fed. Cas. No. 13,466 (C.C.D. Me. 1870) , in which the opinion was given by Mr. Justice Clifford, who was no longer on the bench at the time of the *Boyd* case.

109. 116 U.S. at 622–24. The fact that the order in the *Boyd* case was addressed to Boyd & Sons points up another difference between the order and a search warrant, which traditionally is addressed to the executant official, and authorizes him to search designated premises and seize specified goods, no matter who may be found in possession.

110. 116 U.S. at 624–29.

111. 255 U.S. 298 (1921).

112. Act of June 15, 1917, 40 Stat. 217.

113. This statutory specification of the legitimate scope of federal search warrants is now Rule 41 (b) of the FEDERAL RULES OF CRIMINAL PROCEDURE.

114. 255 U.S. at 306–11.

115. This point was noticed at the time by the late Professor Zechariah Chafee in *The Progress of the Law*, 1919–1922, 35 HARV. L. REV. 673 (1922). The case reached the Supreme Court on questions certified by the Circuit Court of Appeals for the Second Circuit which stated the issue in constitutional terms, and this procedural factor, as Professor Chafee suggests (at 699), may have caused the Court to overlook the warrant's statutory deficiency. However, the questions showed on their face that the warrant had issued under the Espionage Act, and accordingly one would suppose that the well-settled principle of declining unnecessary constitutional decision should have been applied.

116. The case was successfully argued for the defendant by Charles Evans Hughes, a former Associate and future Chief Justice; this circumstance may have helped to keep the rule in good odor until the last few years.

117. *E.g.*, Marron v. United States, 275 U.S. 192 (1927); Harris v. United States, 331 U.S. 145 (1946); Abel v. United States, 362 U.S. 217 (1960).

118. In Thatcher v. Weeks, 79 Me. 457 (1887), the court (at 548–49) supported the arresting officer's right to take from the prisoner "the instruments of the crime and such other articles as may be of use as evidence upon the trial." In Holder v. Hennessey, 141 Mo. 527 (1897), the court likewise recognized (at 540) the ar-

resting officer's authority to search for "all evidence of crime and of identification of the criminal." These appear to be the earliest American cases touching the question in the text.

119. Weeks v. United States, 232 U.S. 383, 392 (1914). The passage quoted is dictum because there was no arrest (and no warrant) to furnish basis for the search. This is the case in which the Supreme Court first applied to the federal courts the exclusionary rule for unlawfully seized evidence.

120. People v. Chiagles, 237 N.Y. 193, 196 (1923).

121. See Harris v. United States, 331 U.S. 145, 154 (1947). The remark here may have been intended to apply only to a search of the *premises* rather than the *person,* in which case it is in line with the course of decisions on this point.

122. Schmerber v. California, 384 U.S. 757 (1966).

123. United States v. Lefkowitz, 285 U.S. 452, 465–66 (1932). This appears to be the only Supreme Court case, other than the *Gouled* case itself, wherein the "mere evidence" rule was applied to exclude evidence seized in a search. In his opinion, Mr. Justice Butler relied (285 U.S. 464) on his assumption that a search of premises pursuant to a valid arrest could not be "greater than that conferred by a search warrant." Obviously, this principle would equally bar seizures of mere evidence from the person of an arrestee.

124. There is an early state court dictum that the premises of an arrested person cannot even be searched, lacking a search warrant, for the fruits of the crime. See Houghton v. Bachman, 47 Barb. 388, 392 (N.Y. Sup. Ct. 1866). Laying aside the spatial limitations to which such a search might be subject, I have found no other support for this view.

125. *Evidentiary Searches: The Rule and the Reason,* 54 GEO. L.J. 593, 605–06 (1966).

126. The presentation quoted in the text closely parallels judicial descriptions of the rule. So far as concerns *instrumentalities* rather than *fruits* of crime, the "possessory" theory relies on the old common-law notion that weapons and other implements of crime are *deodand* and forfeit to the crown. In addition to the "possessory" passages in the *Boyd* (116 U.S. at 623–24) and *Gouled* (255 U.S. at 309) opinions, see United States v. Kirschenblatt, 16 F.2d 202,

203–04 (C.C.A.2d 1926) (L. Hand); People v. Thayer, 63 Cal.2d 635, 408 P.2d 108 (1965)(Traynor).

127. Or, indeed, in or on persons, who may or may not be defendants, if the article sought is situated on a person.

128. 116 U.S. at 626–27 and 630.

129. Elias v. Pasmore (1934) 2 K.B. 164, 50 T.L.R. 196; Dillon v. O'Brien, 16 Cox Crim. Cas. 245 (1887). Counsel for the plaintiff in trespass against the police in the case first cited was Sir Stafford Cripps; the case is discussed and criticized, without reference to the evidentiary character of the documents, in Wade, *Police Search*, 50 LAW Q. REV. 354, 359 (1934).

130. See the *Dillon* case, 16 Cox Crim. Cas. at 251.

131. Official Secrets Act, 1911, c.28, sec. 9.

132. Incitement to Disaffection Act, 1934 § 2, 24 and 25 Geo. 5, c. 56; Betting, Gaming and Lotteries Act, 1963, c.2, § 51.

133. The only pre-*Boyd* case touching on this problem that I have found is Robinson v. Richardson, 13 Gray 454 (Mass. 1859), in which the court (which included Chief Justice Lemuel Shaw) held unconstitutional under the state constitution (the search and seizure provision of which antedated and closely resembles the fourth amendment, *supra* at p. 42) a Massachusetts statute of 1859 authorizing the issuance of search warrants to discover concealed property or assets of a debtor's estate. Judge Merrick wrote (at 456–57): "Search warrants were never recognized by the common law as process which might be availed of by individuals in the course of civil proceedings, or for the maintenance of any private right; but their use was confined to cases of public prosecutions, instituted and pursued for the suppression of crime or the detection and punishment of criminals. . . . Having this knowledge, it cannot be doubted that by the adoption of the 14th article of the Declaration of Rights it was intended strictly and carefully to limit, restrain and regulate the granting and issuing of warrants of that character to the general class of cases, in and to the furtherance of the objects of which they had before been recognized and allowed as justifiable and lawful process, and certainly not so to vary, extend, and enlarge the purposes for and occasions on which they might be used, or to make them available in the course, or for the maintenance, of civil proceedings."

One might quarrel with Judge Merrick's history, insofar as the common-law stolen goods warrant was certainly intended for the relief of the party from whom the goods were stolen, as well as for the apprehension of the thief. Accepting the criminal-civil distinction, however, gives no support to the "mere evidence" restriction, since the evidence is sought and seized for use in a criminal proceeding. *Cf.* Lippman v. People, 175 Ill. 101,51 N.E. 873 (1898).

134. State v. Bisaccia, 45 N.J. 504, 509 (1965): "Indeed, the Fourth and Fifth Amendments are quite incompatible in their immediate operative effect. Whereas the Fifth Amendment forbids the use of any force whatever to compel a person to testify or to produce evidence of his wrong, the Fourth permits the use of all the strength of government to extract from a man's possession things which will convict him."

135. United States v. Poller, 43 F.2d 911, 914 (C.C.A.2d, 1930).

136. United States v. Guido, 251 F.2d 1, 3–4 (C.A.7, 1958).

137. *Eg.,* Marron v. United States, 275 U.S. 192 (1927); Harris v. United States, 331 U.S. 145 (1946); Davis v. United States, 328 U.S. 582 (1946); Abel v. United States, 362 U.S. 217 (1960); Foley v. United States, 64 F.2d 1 (C.C.A.5th, 1933); Matthews v. Conrea, 135 F.2d 524 (C.A.2d, 1943); United States v. Best, 76 F.Supp. 857 (D.Mass. 1948); Leahy v. United States, 272 F.2d 487 (C.A.9th, 1959); United States v. Boyette, 229 F.2d 92 (C.A.4th, 1962).

138. United States v. Kirschenblatt, 16 F.2d 202, 203 (C.C.A.2d, 1926).

139. Gouled v. United States, 255 U.S. 298, 309 (1921).

140. Stanford v. Texas, 379 U.S. 476 (1965).

141. Marcus v. Search Warrants, 367 U.S. 717, 731 (1961); A Quantity of Books v. Kansas, 378 U.S. 205 (1964).

142. United States v. White, 322 U.S. 694, 698 (1944).

143. 116 U.S. at 633.

144. The Parliamentary History of England XVI at 10–11 (1813), proceedings on January 29, 1765.

145. United States v. Poller, 43 F.2d 911, 914 (C.C.A.2d 1930).

146. *E.g.,* Dombrowski v. Pfister, 380 U.S. 479 (1965); Dombrowski v. Eastland, 387 U.S. 82 (196).

147. *Supra* note 99.

148. I recognize that searches and seizures of books and other non-testimonial documents also raise serious questions under the first amendment. See the cases cited *supra* note 141. But it seems to me that the fourth amendment is not the primary instrument of resolution. In other words, *if* we are prepared to accept laws prohibiting the possession of obscene or seditious literature, I suppose that such literature should be subject to search and seizure on proper showing of probable cause and particular description.

149. This is essentially the position taken by the Solicitor General in his brief in the Supreme Court in Warden v. Hayden, 387 U.S. 294 (1967), discussed in the Appendix, *infra* at pp. 93–95. See the brief in that case (No. 480 Oct. Term 1966) for the United States as *amicus curiae,* at 27–29.

150. United States v. Kirschenblatt, 16 F.2d 202, 203 (C.C.A.2d 1926).

151. Quite apart from the question of what things may lawfully be seized pursuant to an otherwise valid search, the general relation between the several types of searches badly needs rationalization. Especially necessary is a basic theory of search incident to arrest. Does it make sense that an arrestee's premises are wholly immune from search if, but only if, the arrest is made elsewhere, as has been the law since Agnello v. United States, 269 U.S. 20 (1925)? It has been suggested that a search incident to arrest should reach so far as is necessary to effect the arrest, but it seems absurd that the thief fleeing with loot from Tiffany's may be searched only for the pistol or knife with which he might resist arrest, and not for the jewelry he has stolen. It seems equally absurd that, if he is chased into and cornered in his or another's abode, those premises should not also be subject to search. On the other side, it also seems unreasonable that, while things seized under a search warrant are returned to the issuing magistrate, those seized incident to arrest remain in police custody; much better that the latter should be accounted for to the arraigning magistrate, and become at once subject to a motion for their return. But all this is another story, and fit material for another lecture.

152. The theory advocated in the text was advanced by Chief Justice Weintraub in State v. Bisaccia, 45 N.J. 504 (1965), wherein he noted (at 513) Lord Camden's emphasis on the invalidity of a "paper search," and concluded (at 515–16) : "There is a marked difference between private papers and other objects in terms of the underlying value the Fourth Amendment seeks to protect." In Hayden v. Warden, 363 F.2d 647 (C.A.4th, 1966), Chief Judge Haynsworth joined in denying the petition for rehearing *en banc,* but noted his view (at 657–58) that while tangible evidentiary articles might legitimately be seized: "a seizure of a diary containing incriminating entries is unreasonable as is a search having as its objective the discovery and seizure of such a document. Each is prohibited by the Fourth and Fourteenth Amendments." See also Judge Haynsworth's earlier and parallel comment in United States v. Boyette, 299 F.2d 92, 95 (L.H.4th, 1962), and Judge Frederick van Pelt Bryan's comparable decision and explanation in United States v. Stern, 225 F.Supp. 187, 192 (S.D.N.Y. 1964).

153. Olmstead v. United States, 277 U.S. 438 (1928).

154. 277 U.S. at 462, 464–65. The Chief Justice also ruled that the fact that the interceptions were violations of the applicable state (Washington) law was not determinative, since at common law illegally obtained evidence is admissible. 277 U.S. at 466–68.

155. Mr. Justice Holmes explicitly passed the constitutional question, and dissented on the sole ground that the interceptions violated Washington law; it was to this aspect of the case, not to wire-tapping in general, that he applied the famous phrase "dirty business." 277 U.S. at 470. Mr. Justice Brandeis dissented on both fourth and fifth amendment grounds, arguing for a broad application of their basic policies in support of man's "right to be let alone —the most comprehensive of rights and the right most valued by civilized men." 277 U.S. at 478. He also joined in the more limited ground taken by Justice Holmes. Mr. Justice Butler dissented on constitutional grounds only, and Mr. Justice Stone concurred with all three of his dissenting brethren. 277 U.S. at 485–88.

156. By section 605 of the Communications Act of 1934, 47 U.S.C. 605.

157. Schwartz v. Texas, 344 U.S. 199 (1952), applied the general rule to wire-tapped evidence.

158. Chief Justice Stone and Justices Frankfurter and Murphy in Goldman v. United States, 316 U.S. 129, 136–37 (1942) ; Justices Douglas, Brennan and Goldberg in Lopez v. United States, 373 U.S. 427, 457–63 (1963).

159. Silverman v. United States, 365 U.S. 505 (1961).

160. Goldman v. United States, 316 U.S. 129 (1942)(6–3); On Lee v. United States, 343 U.S. 747 (1952)(6–3 on the constitutional question); Lopez v. United States, 373 U.S. 427 (1963)(6–3).

161. Mr. Justice Stewart's opinion for the Court is a bit murky on this aspect of the decision, but his reference to an "unauthorized physical penetration" seems to put the case on a trespass footing. 365 U.S. at 509. Justices Clark and Whitaker explicitly grounded their concurrence on the trespass theory, while Justice Douglas equally explicitly rejected it; for him the issue was "whether the privacy of the home was invaded." 365 U.S. at 512–13.

In Irvine v. California, 347 U.S. 178 (1954), where a flagrant trespass was committed in order to install the microphone in the scrutinee's bedroom, the *Wolf* case led to an affirmance of the conviction despite the Court's clearly expressed opinion that such conduct violated the fourth amendment.

With the *Irvine* and *Silverman* cases compare the post-*Mapp* decision in Clinton v. Virginia, 377 U.S. 158 (1954), wherein the state court found that the small prong on the microphone did not penetrate the scrutinee's premises, and that accordingly the *Silverman* case was not controlling. 204 Va. 275, at 282. The Court nevertheless reversed *per curiam* on the authority of the *Silverman* case, and Mr. Justice Clark blithely observed that his concurrence was based on the consideration that the Court found an "actual trespass" to have been committed. It is impossible to contemplate this case without experiencing an almost traumatic sense of confusion.

162. Compare, of course, Griswold v. Connecticut, 381 U.S. 479 (1965).

163. Justices Douglas and Brennan have expressed themselves as favoring the overruling of the *Olmstead* case, *supra* note 158, and the Chief Justice and Justice Fortas might well take the same view.

164. 365 U.S. at 508, 511–12.

165. Cf. Osborn v. United States, 385 U.S. 323 (1966), discussed *infra* at 109. The decision in Berger v. United States, 388 U.S.

41 (1967), in which perhaps the *Olmstead* case was overruled, is discussed *infra* at pp. 100–111.

166. The fifth amendment leg of the *Olmstead* case has weathered the passage of time better than the fourth amendment points. Clandestine surveillance of speech does not constitute compulsion within the meaning of the privilege against self-incrimination. *Cf.* Osborn v. United States, 385 U.S. at 303–04. It might have been thought that Mr. Justice Black's broad conception of the privilege might lead to a contrary conclusion, but he has said nothing to that effect and his concurrences in the fourth amendment decisions discussed above appear to rule it out.

167. A.L.I. Restatement of the Law, Second: Torts Tentative Draft No. 13 § 652 B—Intrusion upon Seclusion.

168. This information is drawn from a memorandum by William H. Crouch of the Library of Congress, printed in *Wiretapping, Eavesdropping, and the Bill of Rights,* Hearing of the Subcommittee on Constitutional Rights of the Senate Committee on the Judiciary on S. Res. 234 (85th Cong. 2d Sess.), Appendix to hearing of May 20, 1958 137 *et seq.* Mr. Crouch's memorandum is based largely on a 1957 Report on interception of communications by a committee of Privy Councillors (reprinted in Part 2 of the hearings, at 459–99), in which it was concluded (para. 39) that, while the original source of authority to open letters was unclear, the power "was exercised widely and publicly known, as the debates in the House of Commons and House of Lords plainly showed."

169. *Ex parte* Jackson, 96 U.S. 727 (1878).

170. *Id.* at 733.

171. The quoted passage from *Ex parte* Jackson was cited with approval in Weeks v. United States, 232 U.S. 383, 390–91 (1914).

172. 277 U.S. at 475.

173. 277 U.S. at 464. This is an intriguing reversal of the British theory that, since the post is a sovereign monopoly, it is open to sovereign interception.

174. Hearings, *supra* note 168, at 35–39. The seven states with anti-bugging laws are California, Illinois, Maryland, Massachusetts, Nevada, New York and Oregon; in Illinois there is no exception for official bugging.

175. Civil Rights Law § 8; N.Y. Const. art I, § 12.

176. Laws 1942 c. 924, effective May 23, 1942, Section 813–a of the Code of Criminal Procedure. Section 813–b, enacted simultaneously, made it a felony for an officer to engage in wire-tapping without the authority provided for in Section 813–a.

177. Laws 1958 c. 676. Minor amendments to the statute were made in 1967. Laws 1967 c. 681 § 86, effective September 1, 1967. In its present form, Section 813–a reads, in relevant part, as follows: "§ 813–a. *Ex parte* order for eavesdropping. An ex parte order for 'wiretapping' or 'mechanical overhearing of a conversation' as defined in . . . the penal law may be issued by any justice of the supreme court or judge of a county court upon oath or affirmation of a district attorney, or of the attorney-general or of an officer above the rank of sergeant of any police department of the state or of any political subdivision thereof, that there is reasonable ground to believe that evidence of crime may be thus obtained, and particularly describing the person or persons whose communications, conversations or discussions are to be overheard or recorded and the purpose thereof, and, in the case of a telegraphic or telephonic communication, identifying the particular telephone number or telegraph line involved. In connection with the issuance of such an order the justice or judge may examine on oath the applicant and any other witness he may produce and shall satisfy himself of the existence of reasonable grounds for the granting of such application."

178. Section 813–a was on this ground held unconstitutional by Judge Nathan Sobel in People v. Grossman, 257 N.Y. Supp.2d 266, 45 Misc.2d 557 (S.Ct. Kings County 1965). The decision is criticized in *Note, Eavesdropping Orders and the Fourth Amendment,* 66 Col. L. Rev. 355 (1966).

179. Kamisar, *Wire-tapping and Eavesdropping: A Professor's View,* 44 Minn. L. Rev. 891 (1960).

180. *Supra* at pp. 68–71. Application here of the testimonial principle might lead to the conclusion that surveillance evidence of "operational" conversations would be admissible, but that such evidence of a conversation in which a gangster boasted to his moll that he had just made a big heist would not be, as that would be like Bluebeard's diary.

181. *E.g.,* Md. Ann. Code, Art. 27, Sec. 125A (1957); Ore. Rev. Stat. Sec. 165.540 (1)(c)(Supp. 1965).

182. *E.g.,* S. 1308 (88th Cong., 1st Sess.), introduced by Senator McClellan on April 10, 1963. Section 5 (b) of the bill provides for application to "a Federal judge of competent jurisdiction," and Section 5 (c) for application to state court judges, for "leave" for law enforcement officials to intercept wire communications in aid of law enforcement. The bill would also authorize wire-tapping without a court order in certain national security cases.

183. COOLEY, CONSTITUTIONAL LIMITATIONS, at 623 (8th ed. 1927).

184. See, *e.g.,* Rule 41 (d) of the FEDERAL RULES OF CRIMINAL PROCEDURE: "The officer taking property under a warrant shall give to the person from whom or from whose premises the property was taken a copy of the warrant and a receipt for the property taken or shall leave the copy and receipt at the place from which the property was taken."

185. HALE, PLEAS OF THE CROWN, *loc. cit. supra* note 16; FED. R. CRIM. P. 41 (d) and (e); Cooley, *op. cit. supra* note 183 at 622.

186. The discussion in the text is directed primarily to surveillance orders for bugging. Of course, if the *Olmstead* case is overruled by holding the telephone network to be a protected private area, these observations would apply equally to wire-tapping.

187. XIX How. St. Trs. 1067. As Lord Chief Justice Pratt, he had voiced the same complaint when charging the jury in Wilkes v. Wood, *supra* note 33.

188. Quincy, *op. cit. supra* note 49, at 471 and 474; Adams papers, *op. cit. supra* note 23, at 125, 128, 139, 142 and 143.

189. The opinions expressed in this and the next succeeding subsection of the text were adumbrated in my letter published in *The Washington Post* on February 12, 1962. The editors of that newspaper were not converted to my views. See also, in general agreement with my position, the statement of the late Thomas McBride, Attorney General of Pennsylvania, Hearings, *supra* note 168, Part I, p. 26.

190. JACKSON, THE SUPREME COURT IN THE AMERICAN SYSTEM OF GOVERNMENT at 12 (1955). This paper had been intended for delivery as a Godkin lecture at Harvard University.

191. See the cases and comments in HART AND WECHSLER, CASES

AND MATERIALS ON FEDERAL JURISDICTION at 95–156 and 213–17 (1953).

192. For other expressions of this view, in addition to Mr. Justice Jackson's, see the testimonies of John P. Walsh (Chairman of the Committee on Criminal Justice and Law Enforcement of the Philadelphia Bar Association) in *Wiretapping*, Hearings of Subcommittee No. 57 of the House Committee on the Judiciary (845h Cong., 1st Sess., 1955) at 339; of Murray A. Gordon of the National Lawyers Guild, *id.* at 234–39; of Charles A. Reich, Professor at the Yale Law School, in Wiretapping and Eavesdropping Legislation, Hearings of Subcommittee on Constitutional Rights of the Senate Judiciary Committee (87th Cong., 1st Sess. 1961) at 183–84; of Herman Schwarz of the American Civil Liberties Union, *id.* at 411.

193. Tutun v. United States, 270 U.S. 568 (1926).

194. Veeder v. United States, 252 Fed. 414 (C.C.A. 7th, 1918), cert. den. 246 U.S. 675; see United States v. Wallace Co., 336 U.S. 793, 802 (1949); *cf.* Cogen v. United States, 278 U.S. 200 (1928); In re 14 East Seventeenth St., 65 F.2d 289 (C.C.A.2d 1933); United States v. Maresca, 266 Fed. 713 (S.D.N.Y. 1920).

195. Conceivably it is possible so to draw a surveillance order statute as to give the scrutinee, in every case, a right at some point to challenge the order in a judicial proceeding. Generally, however, he is given only the right to move to suppress evidence in connection with a criminal trial, so that if he is not to be tried, he has no recourse and, in all probability, remains in ignorance that he has been the object of surveillance.

196. On the necessity of opportunity to challenge, *cf.* People v. Holcomb, 3 Park C.C. 656 (N.Y. Sup. Ct. 1858), in which the court declared (at 668) that "it was never contemplated that a search warrant should be issued to obtain possession of property alleged to have been stolen, and when brought to the justice that he should order it to be delivered over to the person claiming to be the owner, upon *ex parte* proof of his title. No freeman can be thus dispossessed of property. He is entitled to a day in court, a hearing in some tribunal, before his possession is disturbed."

197. Siegel v. People, 16 N.Y.2d 330 (1960). Judges Burke and Scileppi thought the order under Section 813–a unreviewable; Judges Dye and Bergan concurred in the result on the ground that the order was unreviewable in the Court of Appeals, and reviewable

below only at the discretion of the Appellate Division, where the petition to vacate the order had been filed. Judges Desmond, Fuld, and Van Voorhis dissented on the ground that the order was reviewable, citing the *Silverman* case and Griswold v. Connecticut, *supra* notes 159 and 162 respectively. *Cf.* People v. McCall, 17 N.Y.2d 152 (1966).

198. Conflicting testimony on this point was given in 1955 by the District Attorney of New York County (the Honorable Frank Hogan) and a former member of his staff, William J. Keating. Hearings, *supra* note 3 at 189–94 and 323–24.

199. Hearings, *supra* note 3 at 476.

200. *Supra* at pp. 68–71.

201. See Mr. Justice Murphy's dissenting opinion in Goldman v. United States, 316 U.S. 129, 139–40 (1942) ; Mr. Justice Brennan's dissenting opinion, concurred in by Justices Douglas and Goldberg, in Lopez v. United States, 373 U.S. 427, 466–71 (1963).

202. Osborn v. United States, 385 U.S. 323, 353 (1966).

203. *Supra* note 201.

204. *Supra* note 202. Mr. Justice White took no part, and Mr. Justice Douglas dissented.

205. The *Osborn* case was like the *Lopez* case in that the informer wore a concealed recording device. No trespassory surveillance was involved. The recording was authorized in the course of the trial of James R. Hoffa in Nashville, in order to determine whether efforts were being made to corrupt jurors. Therefore, although a federal case, it raised no article III case and controversy problem.

206. People v. Berger, 18 N.Y.2d 638 (1966), *cert. granted* December 5, 1966, No. 615, October Term 1966. The Supreme Court's decision, 388 U.S. 41 (1967), is discussed in the Appendix, *infra* at pp. 110–11.

Part II

1. Act of March 2, 1831, 44 Stat. 487. Its constitutionality as applied to the lower federal courts, was upheld in *Ex parte* Robinson, 19 Wall. 505 (1873).

2. 18 U.S.C. 401 (1964).

3. For a discussion of the origins and questionable ancestry of this practice, see Fox, THE HISTORY OF CONTEMPT OF COURT 5–15 (1927) ; Frankfurter and Landis, *Power to Regulate Contempts,* 37 HARV. L REV. 1010, 1048–50 (1924). The source of the historical controversy is Mr. Justice Wilmot's opinion in Rex v. Almon, Wilm. 243, 97 Eng. Rep. 94 (1765). A useful memorandum describing the leading modern English decisions in this field is attached to Mr. Justice Frankfurter's opinion in Maryland v. Baltimore Radio Show, Inc., 338 U.S. 912, 921–36 (1950).

4. The phrase "near thereto" was contemporaneously construed as geographical rather than causative. *Ex parte Poulson* 19 Fed. Cas. 1205 (No. 11350) (C.C.E.D.Pa. 1835). In 1918 the Supreme Court adopted a causative interpretation and sustained a contempt judgment against a Toledo newspaper for objectionable comments on a pending proceeding. Toledo Newspaper v. United States, 247 U.S. 419 (1918). But the *Toledo* case was overruled, and the geographical sense reaffirmed, in Nye v. United States, 313 U.S. 33 (1941).

5. District Judge James H. Peck of Missouri, who had summarily punished the author of a critical article about his conduct of land grant adjudication proceedings, was acquitted by a vote of 22–21. The bill which became the 1831 statute was introduced shortly thereafter. It was comparable to laws previously enacted in Pennsylvania and New York, and after 1831 a large number of other states followed suit. GOLDFARB, THE CONTEMPT POWER 20–22 (1963).

6. Standards Relating to Fair Trial and Free Press, American Bar Association Project on Minimum Standards for Criminal Justice —Tentative Draft Recommended by the Advisory Committee on Fair Trial and Free Press (1966).

7. *Id.* at 21, quoting *Trial by Jury in New York,* 9 L. Rep. 193, 198 (1846).

8. United States v. Holmes, Fed. Cas. No. 15,383 (C.C.E.D.Pa. 1842). The other is Regina v. Dudley and Stephens, L.R. 14 Q.B.D. 273 (1884).

9. The story of the sinking of the *William Brown,* and of the ensuing events and the trial in Philadelphia, is told in HICKS, HUMAN JETTISON (1927).

10. *Trial by Newspapers,* 14 Crim. Law Mag. 550 (1892), from an address delivered March 31, 1892 before the Sunset Club of Chicago by William S. Forrest, Esq.

11. J.W.G., *Trial by Newspapers,* I Journal of the American Institute of Criminal Law and Criminology No. 6, at 849–51 (Mar. 1911).

12. The recommendations are set forth in 22 A.B.A. Journal 79–80 (Feb. 1936). The members were Dean Albert J. Harno of the University of Illinois and three practicing lawyers—Oscar Hallam of Minneapolis, John Kirkland Clark of New York, and Charles P. Taft of Cincinnati.

13. Estes v. Texas, 381 U.S. 532 (1965).

14. The rules are set out in full in the Report of the 45th Annual Meeting of the Maryland State Bar Association (1940) at 134. They met their demise ten years later, when the Supreme Court of Maryland reversed a contempt conviction under the rules, on the authority of the Supreme Court's decisions in Bridges v. California, 314 U.S. 252 (1947) and Pennekamp v. Florida, 328 U.S. 331 (1946). The Supreme Court denied certiorari in the Maryland case. Baltimore Radio Show v. State, 193 Md. 300, 67 A.2d 497 (1949), *cert. den.* 338 U.S. 912 (1950), *supra* note 3.

15. People v. Jelke, 308 N.Y. 56, 123 N.E.2d 769 (1954).

16. 11 N.Y. County Law. Ass'n Bar Bull. 96 (1953).

17. Bridges v. California and Pennekamp v. Florida, *supra* note 14; Craig v. Harney, 331 U.S. 331 (1946); Wood v. Georgia, 370 U.S. 375 (1962). In addition, the Court denied certiorari in the Maryland case, *supra* notes 3 and 14.

18. Marshall v. United States, 360 U.S. 310 (1959); Irvin v. Dowd, 366 U.S. 717 (1961); Rideau v. Louisiana, 373 U.S. 723 (1963); Estes v. Texas, *supra* note 13; Sheppard v. Maxwell, 384 U.S. 364 (1966).

19. Report of the President's Commission on the Assassination of President John F. Kennedy, at 240–42 (1964).

20. See Sheppard v. Maxwell, 384 U.S. at 357–63.

21. Judge Paschen had denied the newspapers acess to transcripts of the *voir dire* and forbidden them to report the questions and

answers on *voir dire* or the names of the jurors or to make any court-room sketches. In a five to one ruling, the Supreme Court of Illinois ordered that reporting of all proceedings in open court be permitted, but upheld the ban on reporting jurors' names until they were either excused or sworn. See the accounts in The New York Times of February 24th and March 1st and 2nd, 1967. More moderate restrictions, unchallenged by the press, had been imposed in the Gallashaw murder trial in New York City by Justice Julius Helfand. The New York Times, Oct. 4, 1966.

22. State v. Van Duyne, 43 N.J. 369, 204 A.2d 841 (1964). Compare the action of two Superior Court judges in Raleigh, North Carolina, who issued orders forbidding attorneys, police officers, or any persons connected with the court from giving out information concerning confessions, criminal records, or anticipated evidence. The New York Times, Sept. 14 and 18, 1966.

23. 28 C.F.R. § 50.2 (1965).

24. The New York Times, Dec. 7, 1964 and March 14, 1965.

25. The newspapers subscribing to this code are *The Toledo Blade* and *The Toledo Times*. See The New York Times, Aug. 22, 1966.

26. The Columbia "guidelines" are set forth in full in an appendix to Taylor, *Crime Reporting and Publicity of Criminal Proceedings,* 66 Col. L. Rev. 34, at 60 (1966).

27. Since this "guide" is commendably comprehensive and embodies an unusual consensus, I have reproduced it, in principal part, below:

MASSACHUSETTS GUIDE FOR THE BAR AND NEWS MEDIA

1. *Guide for Press*

Preamble

1. To promote closer understanding between the bar and the press, especially in their efforts to reconcile the constitutional guarantee of freedom of the press and the right to a fair, impartial trial, the following mutual and voluntary statement of principles is recommended to all members of both professions.

2. Both professions, recognizing that freedom of the press is one of the fundamental liberties guaranteed by the First Amendment to the United States Constitution, agree that this fundamental freedom must be zealously preserved and responsibly exercised subject only to those restrictions designed to safeguard equally fundamental rights of the individual.

3. It is likewise agreed that both the press and the bar are obliged to preserve the principle of the presumption of innocence for those accused of wrongdoing pending a finding of guilty.

4. The press and the bar concur on the importance of the natural right of the members of an organized society to acquire and impart information about their common interests.

5. It is further agreed, however, that the inherent right of society's members to impart and acquire information should be exercised with discretion at those times when public disclosures would jeopardize the ends of justice, public security and other rights of individuals.

6. The press and the bar recognize that there may arise circumstances in which disclosures of names of individuals involved in matters coming to the attention of the general public would result in personal danger, harm to the reputation of a person or persons or notoriety to an innocent third party.

7. Consistent with the principles of this preamble, it is the responsibility of the bar, no less than that of the press, to support the free flow of information.

For the Press

Newspapers in publishing accounts of crimes should keep in mind that the accused may be tried in a court of law.

To preserve the individual's rights to a fair trial, news stories of crime should contain only a factual statement of the arrest and attending circumstances.

The following should be avoided:

1. Publication of interviews with subpoenaed witnesses after an indictment is returned.

2. Publication of the criminal record or discreditable acts of the accused after an indictment is returned or during the trial unless made part of the evidence in the court record. The defendant is being tried on the charge for which he is accused and not on his record. (Publication of a criminal record could be grounds for a libel suit.)

3. Publication of confessions after an indictment is returned unless made a part of the evidence in the court record.

4. Publication of testimony stricken by the court, unless reported as having been stricken.

5. Editorial comment preceding or during trial, tending to influence judge or jury.

6. Publication of names of juveniles involved in juvenile proceedings unless the names are released by the judge.

7. The publication of any "leaks," statements or conclusions as to the innocence or guilt, implied or expressed, by the police or prosecuting authorities or defense counsel.

2. *Guide for Broadcasting Industry*

. . . [The "Guide" for the "broadcast news media" incorporates in nearly identical language the principles proposed to govern the conduct of the "press."]

3. *Guide for the Bar*

To preserve the individual's rights to a fair trial in a court of law the following guidelines are prescribed for the Bar.

1. A factual statement of the arrest and circumstances and incidents thereof of a person charged with a crime is permissible, but the following should be avoided:

   (A) Statements or conclusions as to the innocence or guilt, implied or expressed, by the prosecuting authorities or defense counsel.

   (B) Out-of-court statements by prosecutors or defense attorneys to news media in advance of or during trial, stating what they expect to prove, whom they propose to call as witnesses or public criticism of either judge or jury.

(C) Issuance by the prosecuting authorities, counsel for the defense or any person having official connection with the case of any statements relative to the conduct of the accused, statements, "confessions" or admissions made by the accused or other matters bearing on the issue to be tried.

(D) Any other statement or press release to the news media in which the source of the statement remains undisclosed.

2. At the same time, in the interest of fair and accurate reporting, news media have a right to expect the cooperation of the authorities in facilitating adequate coverage of the law enforcement process.

28. POPULAR GOVERNMENT, at 21–26 (April 1967). This is a publication of the Institute of Government, at the University of North Carolina.

29. Report of Press-Bar committee, American Society of Newspaper Editors, 1964–65, unanimously approved by the Board of Directors of the Society on April 14, 1965, and hereinafter cited as ASNE Report. The chairman of the Committee was Alfred Friendly, the managing editor of The Washington Post, and the other members were Creed C. Black, managing editor of The Chicago Daily News, Herbert Brucker, editorial-page editor of The Hartford Courant, and Felix B. McNight, editor of The Dallas Times-Herald.

30. Free Press and Fair Trial, American Newspaper Publishers Association (1965), hereinafter cited as ANPA Report.

31. Standards Relating to Fair Trial and Free Press, *supra* note 6, hereinafter cited as ABA Report.

32. Freedom of the Press and Fair Trial—Final Report with Recommendations, Special Committee on Radio, Television and the Administration of Justice of the Association of the Bar of the City of New York (1967), hereinafter cited as ABNY Report. An earlier report by the same committee is Radio, Television and the Administration of Justice—A Documented Survey of Materials (1965).

The Philadelphia Bar Association in 1964 adopted a "Statement of Policy" which caused intense local debate but has not become a focus of national discussion. See The New York Times, Dec. 20, 29, 30, and 31, 1964, and Jan. 15 and 29, 1965. Another such statement, joined in by some press representatives but not by the three major Philadelphia dailies, was adopted by the Association November 9, 1965. See The New York Times, October 24 and November 11, 1965.

33. Since the delivery of this address, another report on the subject has been published by a committee on the Judicial Conference of the United States, headed by Judge Irving R. Kaufman, of the Court of Appeals for the Second Circuit. I have commented on this report in an Appendix, *infra* at 000–00.

34. TEX. CODE OF CRIM. PROC. art. 38.11 (Vernon's Ann. 1966). Under this provision, husbands and wives may testify for but not against each other in criminal prosecutions.

35. ABA Report at 25–47.

36. ANPA Report at 2.

37. ASNE Report at 2.

38. HARRY KALVEN and HANS ZEIL, THE AMERICAN JURY (1966).

39. On January 13, 1968 the ANPA Foundation announced its commissioning of a "major study" of this question, financed by a grant from the Robert R. McCormick Charitable Trust. The New York Times, Jan. 4, 1968. The techniques to be used include numerous interviews of state criminal court judges, and an "extensive literature search." The application of these techniques may well yield helpful information, but hardly can be conclusive; nor can the auspices be regarded as wholly unprejudiced, in view of the positions already taken by the ANPA itself.

40. ABA Report at 23–24 and 252–58.

41. Stanton, *Justice and the News Media,* in TRIAL (Dec./Jan. 1967) at 41.

42. The Columbia Project for Effective Justice has been hoping to conduct just such a study through the Bureau of Applied Research, but the techniques are complicated and financing is not presently available.

43. The New York Times, March 11 and 31, 1967.

44. Note, 34 N.Y.U.L. Rev. 1278, 1290 n.78 (1955).

45. Irvin v. Dowd, *supra* note 18. See also the cases described in the ABA Report at 58–59, including Geagan v. Gavin, 292 F.2d 244 (C.A.1, 1961), in which 1104 jurors were examined, 659 declared that they had already formed an opinion, and the first juror was accepted on the 30th day of *voir dire*.

46. ASNE Report at 3.

47. ABA Report at 159–89 and 192–227.

48. *Supra* at pp. 126–27.

49. ABA Report at 164.

50. ANPA Report at 9.

51. Warren Report at 240.

52. ASNE Report at 11–12.

53. ANPA Report at 1.

54. *Ibid.*

55. ASNE Report at 8.

56. ANPA Report at 5.

57. ABA Report at 47–51.

58. People v. Whittemore, 45 Misc. 2d 506, 257 N.Y.S.2d 787 (Sup. Ct. 1965).

59. Taylor, *supra* note 26, 66 Col. L. Rev. at 48–51.

60. 384 U.S. at 350.

61. *Supra* notes 31 and 32.

62. ABA Report at 2–5 and 80–97; ABNY Report at 14–26. In New Jersey, the *Van Duyne* rules (*supra* at pp. 126–27 and note 22) achieve much the same result by interpretation of the present language of Canon 20.

63. ABA Report at 4–5 and 96–97.

64. ABNY Report at 44–45.

65. ABA Report at 28–30 and 195 and 203.

66. ABA Report at 5–8 and 98–111; ABNY Report at 27–35 and 39–43.

67. ABNY Report at 39–47.

68. ABA Report at 14–15 and 150–55.

69. ABNY Report at 40.

70. *Id.* at 27 and 40. The ANPA Report, which makes the same point (at 8), invokes the separation of powers.

71. *Id.* at 42: "In State v. Van Duyne . . . [*supra* note 22] it was said that the matter is 'largely in the hands of the prosecutor and local police authorities.' In State v. Thompson, 139 N.W.2d 490 (Minn. 1966), the court remarked: 'Police officers, over whom we have no such disciplinary power, might like more to be dealt with by their superior officers.' 139 N.W.2d at 514." Both of these dicta are *en passant* rather than considered. The Report also cites a comment in Mr. Justice Clark's opinion in the *Sheppard* case, *supra* note 20, which seems entirely irrelevant.

72. ABA Report at 5.

73. *Id.* at 102–106.

74. United States v. Shipp, 203 U.S. 563 (1906).

75. Rea v. United States, 350 U.S. 214 (1956).

76. ABA Report at 102.

77. ABNY Report at 39 and 40.

78. ABNY Report at 32–35.

79. In the *Sheppard* case, the Court merely noted, 389 U.S. at 358: "We do not consider what sanctions might be available against a recalcitrant press. . . ." In Wood v. Georgia the Court remarked (370 U.S. at 389–90) that ". . . the limitations on free speech assume a different proportion where expression is directed toward a trial as compared to a grand jury investigation."

80. The foundational case is Roach v. Garvan, 2 Atk. 469, 26 Eng. Rep. 683 (Ch. 1742), in which Lord Hardwicke committed to the Fleet the printer of the *St. James's Evening Post* for prejudicial comments on the witnesses in a pending case. See also Lord Ellenborough's remarks in Rex v. Fisher, 11 R.R.799 (K.B. 1811); Goodhart, *Newspapers and Contempt of Court,* 48 Harv. L. Rev. 885, 887–88 (1935).

81. Levy, Legacy of Suppression (1960), *passim.*

82. Hollingsworth v. Duane, Fed. Cas. No. 6616 (C.C.Pa.1801).

83. Act of Feb. 23, 1801, 2 Stat. 89. The court in the Hollingsworth case comprised William Tilghman of Pennsylvania, Chief Judge, and William Griffith of New Jersey, both of whom held office only briefly, until the repeal of the statute on March 8, 1802, 2 Stat. 132.

84. Respublica v. Oswald, 1 Dall. 318 (S. Ct. Pa. 1788).

85. Bridges v. California, 314 U.S. 252 (1941).

86. *Eg.*, Globe Newspaper v. Commonwealth, 188 Mass. 449, 74 N.E. 682 (1905); Bee Publishing Co. v. State, 107 Neb. 74, 185 N.W. 339 (1921); Tate v. State, 132 Tenn. 131, 177 S.W. 69 (1915); Publishing Co. v. Lewis, 42 Utah 188, 129 Pac. 624 (1913).

87. *Supra* at pp. 122–23.

88. Gitlow v. New York, 268 U.S. 652 (1925), is generally regarded as the point of origin of first amendment limitations on the states. DeJonge v. Oregon, 299 U.S. 353 (1937), Herndon v. Lowry, 301 U.S. 242 (1937), Lovell v. Griffin, 303 U.S. 444 (1938), Cantwell v. Connecticut, 310 U.S. 296 (1940), and Thornhill v. Alabama, 310 U.S. 88 (1940) are among the first amendment decisions which shortly preceded the *Bridges* case.

89. See *Justice Black and First Amendment Absolutes: A Public Interview,* 37 N.Y.U. L. Rev. 549, 563 (1962).

90. The cases subsequent to the *Bridges* case, in all of which the contempt convictions were reversed by the Court, are Pennekamp v. Florida, 328 U.S. 331 (1946), Craig v. Harvey, 331 U.S. 367 (1947), and Wood v. Georgia, 370 U.S. 375 (1962). In addition the Court denied certiorari in the *Baltimore Radio Show* case, in which the Maryland Supreme Court set aside the contempt conviction under the "Tarquinio rules," *supra* at pp. 122–23 and note 14.

91. The murder case involved in *Baltimore Radio Show, supra* note 90, was tried before a judge, apparently because defense counsel feared the adverse effect of the pre-trial publicity on a jury.

92. *Op. cit. supra* note 89.

93. Opinion of the Justices, 349 Mass. 786, 208 N.E.2d 240 (1965).

94. 314 U.S. at 260, and 370 U.S. at 385–86.

95. Ferguson v. Georgia, 365 U.S. 570, 582 (1961), discussed *supra* at p. 7.

96. Such appears to be the timid thrust of Opinion of the Justices, *supra* note 93. A few trial courts still venture occasional use of the contempt power against the press. See, e.g., The New York Times, November 6, 1966, reporting such an instance in Springfield, Massachusetts, and January 18, 1966, in New Martinsville, West Virginia. A like proceeding in Phoenix, Arizona was halted by a writ of prohibition from the Supreme Court of Arizona, according to The New York Times, January 6, 1966.

97. ABNY Report at 13.

98. This is the bill considered in Opinion of the Justices, *supra* note 93. See the discussion in the ABA Report at 69.

99. ABNY Report at 13.

100. The last clause is based on the writer's personal consultation with Mr. Hogan.

101. ABA Report at 164.

102. *Id.* at 162, 165, and 190–91.

103. *Id.* at 159–71.

104. ABA Report at 164.

105. In this respect there is a remarkable but perhaps accidental difference between the ABA and ABNY recommendations with respect to Canon 20. The former apply to a member of the bar only "in connection with pending or imminent criminal litigation with which he is associated." ABA Report at 2. The latter applies to "members of the bar," without limitation to those associated with the particular case. ABNY Report at 20.

106. ABNY Report at 20.

107. The New York Times, December 4, 1965.

Index

INDEX

Acts: Licensing, 25, 33; Official Secrets, 62; "midnight judges" act, 159

Adams, John, *see* "midnight judges" act

Adjudication, constitutional, 4

Agencies: news: self-regulation by, 129–30; governmental: self-regulation by, 128–29

American Bar Association (ABA): Hauptmann trial, 122; on free press, 148

ABA Report, *see* Fair trial and free press: Report by the Committee on the Operation of the Jury System . . . of the United States

American Law Institute, 15; Model Code of Pre-Arraignment Procedure, 3–4

American Society of Newspaper Editors (ASNE), 125, 130, 134; ASNE Report, *see* Fair trial and free press

American Telephone and Telegraph Company, 72

Association of the Bar of the City of New York (ABNY) Report, *see* Fair trial and free press

Attainder, Bill of: *see* Lovett v. *United States*

Baldwin, Justice, 120–21

Bathurst, First Earl of, *see* Wilkes and *Entick* cases

Bench, King's, 36

Berger v. *New York,* 6, n. 10, 100–102, 104, 107–108, 110–12

Berkshire Eagle, adherence to Massachusetts bar-press code, 165

Bill of Rights, *see* Constitution, U.S.

Black, Hugo, Assoc. Justice, U.S. Supreme Court: on American Law Institute Model Code, 3–8, 11–12; *Berger* v. *New York,* 100–101; *Bridges* case, the, 160–62; eighth amendment, 14–15; first amendment, 147; fourth amendment and search and seizure, 20; *Katz* v. *United States,* 111–12; *Mapp* case and the fifth amendment, 107; *Olmstead* case, 103; *Warren* v. *Hayden,* 94

Bluebeard's Diary, 64–65, 69

Boyd v. *United States,* 53, 56, 60–62, 67, 70

Bradley, Justice, *see* *Boyd* v. *United States*

Brandeis, Louis, Assoc. Justice, U.S. Supreme Court: *Olmstead* v. United States, 72, 76; adversity of parties, 86, n. 193

Brennan, William Joseph, Assoc. Justice, U.S. Supreme Court: Georgia statute, view of, 7, 19; "mere evidence" rule, 94–95; surveillance problems, 92, 102

Bridges v. *California,* 123, n. 17; cited, 149–50; "clear and present danger" test, applied to,

Index

Index

Index

Index

Index

Index

Index

Index